Project Management (PjM)

ARE 5 Mock Exam
(Architect Registration Examination)

ARE 5 Overview, Exam Prep Tips,
Hotspots, Case Studies, Drag-and-Place,
Solutions and Explanations

Gang Chen

ArchiteG®, Inc.
Irvine, California

Project Management (PjM) ARE 5.0 Mock Exam (Architect Registration Examination): ARE 5.0 Overview, Exam Prep Tips, Hotspots, Case Studies, Drag-and-Place, Solutions and Explanations

Copyright © 2018	Gang Chen
V6	
Cover Photo © 2018	Gang Chen
Copy Editor:	Penny L Kortje

ArchiteG®, Inc.
http://www.ArchiteG.com

ISBN: 978-1-61265-037-1

PRINTED IN THE UNITED STATES OF AMERICA

What others are saying about *ARE Mock Exam series* ...

"Great study guide..."

"This was a great resource supplement to my other study resources. I appreciated the mock exam questions the most, and the solutions offer an explanation as to why the answer is correct. I will definitely check out his other ARE exam resources!

UPDATE: Got my PASS Letter!"
—**Sean Primeaux**

"Tried everything 4 times before reading this book and PASSED!"

"I had failed this exam 4 times prior to getting this book...I had zero clue as to what I was doing wrong. I read Ballast, Kaplan and random things on the forum but for the life of me couldn't pin point where I was missing it until I read THIS BOOK! Gang did an excellent job...I remember going through the ramp and reading Gang's book and saying Ohhhh like 4 or 5 times. I read his book several times until I became comfortable with the information. I went in on test day and it was a breeze. I remember walking out of there thinking I couldn't believe I struggled so much before. The tips in here are priceless! I strongly recommend this book..."
—**hendea1**

"Add this to your ARE study"

"This was a very helpful practice exam and discussion. I really appreciated the step-by-step review of the author's approach... As I studied it last before taking the test, Gang Chen's book probably made the difference for me."
—**Dan Clowes ("XLine")**

"Good supplemental mock exam"

"I found the mock exam to be very helpful, all of the answers are explained thoroughly and really help you understand why it is correct...Also the introduction and test taking tips are very helpful for new candidates just starting the ARE process."
—**Bgrueb01**

"Essential Study Tool"

"I have read the book and found it to be a great study guide for myself. Mr. Gang Chen does such a great job of helping you get into the right frame of mind for the content of the exam. Mr. Chen breaks down the points on what should be studied and how to improve your chances of a pass with his knowledge and tips for the exam.

I highly recommend this book to anyone...it is an invaluable tool in the preparation for the exam as Mr. Chen provides a vast amount of knowledge in a very clear, concise, and logical matter."
—**Luke Giaccio**

"Wish I had this book earlier"
"...The questions are written like the NCARB questions, with various types...check all that apply, fill in the blank, best answer, etc. The answer key helpfully describes why the correct answer is correct, and why the incorrect answers are not. Take it from my experience, at half the cost of other mock exams, this is a must buy if you want to pass..."
—Domiane Forte ("Vitruvian Duck")

"This book did exactly like the others said."
"This book did exactly like the others said. It is immensely helpful with the explanation... There are so many codes to incorporate, but Chen simplifies it into a methodical process. Bought it and just found out I passed. I would recommend."
—Dustin

"It was the reason I passed."
"This book was a huge help. I passed the AREs recently and I felt this book gave me really good explanations for each answer. It was the reason I passed."
—Amazon Customer

"Great Practice Exam"
"… For me, it was difficult to not be overwhelmed by the amount of content covered by the Exam. This Mock Exam is the perfect tool to keep you focused on the content that matters and to evaluate what you know and what you need to study. It definitely helped me pass the exam!!"
—Michael Harvey ("Harv")

"One of the best practice exams"
"Excellent study guide with study tips, general test info, and recommended study resources. Hands down one of the best practice exams that I have come across for this exam. Most importantly, the practice exam includes in depth explanations of answers. Definitely recommended."
—Taylor Cupp

"Great Supplement!!"
"This publication was very helpful in my preparation for my BS exam. It contained a mock exam, followed by the answers and brief explanations to the answers. I would recommend this as an additional study material for this exam."
—Cynthia Zorrilla-Canteros ("czcante")

"Fantastic! "
"When I first began to prepare for this exam; the number of content areas seemed overwhelming and daunting at best. However, this guide clearly dissected each content area into small management components. Of all the study guides currently available for this test - this exam not only included numerous resources (web links, you tube clips, etc..), but also the sample test was extremely helpful. The sample test incorporated a nice balance of diagrams, calculations and general concepts - this book allowed me to highlight any "weak" content areas I had prior to the real exam. In short - this is an awesome book!"
—Rachel Casey (RC)

Dedication

To my parents, Zhuixian and Yugen,
my wife Yongqing Fang, and my daughters,
Alice, Angela, Amy, and Athena.

Disclaimer

ARE Mock Exam series by ArchiteG, Inc.

Time and effort is the most valuable asset of a candidate. How to cherish and effectively use your limited time and effort is the key of passing any exam. That is why we publish the ARE Mock Exam series to help you to study and pass the ARE exams in the shortest time possible. We have done the hard work so that you can save time and money. We do not want to make you work harder than you have to. To save your time, we use a *standard* format for all our ARE 5.0 Mock Exam books, so that you can quickly skip the *identical* information you have already read in other books of the series, and go straight to the *unique* "meat and potatoes" portion of the book.

The trick and the most difficult part of writing a good book is to turn something that is very complicated into something that is very simple. This involves researching and really understanding some very complicated materials, absorbing the information, and then writing about the topic in a way that makes it very easy to understand. To succeed at this, you need to know the materials very well. Our goal is to write books that are clear, concise, and helpful to anyone with a seventh-grade education.

Do not force yourself to memorize a lot of numbers. Read through the numbers a few times, and you should have a very good impression of them.

You need to make the judgment call: If you miss a few numbers, you can still pass the exam, but if you spend too much time drilling these numbers, you may miss out on the big pictures and fail the exam.

The existing ARE practice questions or exams by others are either way too easy or way over-killed. They do NOT match the real ARE 5.0 exams at all.

We have done very comprehensive research on the official NCARB guides, many related websites, reference materials, and other available ARE exam prep materials. We match our mock exams as close as possible to the NCARB samples and the real ARE exams instead. Some readers had failed an ARE exam two or three times before, and they eventually passed the exam with our help.

All our books include a complete set of questions and case studies. We try to mimic the real ARE exams by including the same number of questions, using a similar format, and asking the same type of questions. We also include detailed answers and explanations to our questions.

There is some extra information on ARE overviews and exam-taking tips in Chapter One. This is based on NCARB *and* other valuable sources. This is a bonus feature we included in each book because we want our readers to be able to buy our ARE mock exam books together or individually. We want you to find all necessary ARE exam information and resources at one place and through our books.

All our books are available at
http://www.GreenExamEducation.com

How to Use This Book

We suggest you read *Project Management (PjM) ARE 5.0 Mock Exam (Architect Registration Examination)* at least three times:

Read once and cover Chapter One and Two, the Appendixes, the related *free* PDF files, and other resources. Highlight the information you are not familiar with.

Read twice focusing on the highlighted information to memorize. You can repeat this process as many times as you want until you master the content of the book.

After reviewing these materials, you can take the mock exam, and then check your answers against the answers and explanations in the back, including explanations for the questions you answer correctly. You may have answered some questions correctly for the wrong reason. Highlight the information you are not familiar with.

Like the real exam, the mock exam will continue to use **multiple choice, check-all-that-apply,** and **quantitative fill-in-the-blank**. There are also three new question types: **Hotspots, case studies,** and **drag-and-place**.

Review your highlighted information, and take the mock exam again. Try to answer 100% of the questions correctly this time. Repeat the process until you can answer all the questions correctly.

Project Management is one of the most difficult ARE divisions because some questions require calculations. This book includes most if not all the information you need to do the calculations, as well as step-by-step explanations. After reading this book, you will greatly improve your ability to deal with the real ARE calculations, and have a great chance of passing the exam on the first try.

Take the mock exam at least two weeks before the real exam. You should definitely NOT wait until the night before the real exam to take the mock exam. If you do not do well, you will go into panic mode and NOT have enough time to review your weaknesses.

Read for the final time the night before the real exam. Review ONLY the information you highlighted, especially the questions you did not answer correctly when you took the mock exam for the first time.

This book is very light so you can easily carry it around. These features will allow you to review the book whenever you have a few minutes.

The Table of Contents is very detailed so you can locate information quickly. If you are on a tight schedule you can forgo reading the book linearly and jump around to the sections you need.

All our books, including "ARE Mock Exams Series" and "LEED Exam Guides Series," are available at
GreenExamEducation.com

Check out FREE tips and info at **GeeForum.com**, you can post your questions for other users' review and responses.

Table of Contents

Chapter One   Overview of Architect Registration Examination (ARE)

   1. Important links to the FREE and official NCARB documents
   2. A detailed list and brief description of the FREE PDF files that you can download from NCARB
      - ARE 5.0 Credit Model
      - ARE 5.0 Guidelines
      - NCARB Education Guidelines
      - Architectural Experience Program (AXP) Guidelines
      - Certification Guidelines
      - ARE 5.0 Related FAQs (Frequently Asked Questions)
      - Your Guide to ARE 5.0
      - ARE 5.0 Handbook
      - ARE 5.0 Test Specification
      - ARE 5.0 Prep Videos
      - The Burning Question: Why do we need an ARE anyway?
      - Defining Your Moral Compass
      - Rules of Conduct

   1. What is IDP? What is AXP?
   2. Who qualifies as an intern?

Chapter Two   Project Management (PjM) Division

Back Page Promotion
  A. ARE Mock Exam series (GreenExamEducation.com)
  B. LEED Exam Guides series (GreenExamEducation.com)
  C. *Building Construction* (ArchiteG.com)
  D. *Planting Design Illustrated*

Index

Chapter One

Overview of the Architect Registration Examination (ARE)

A. First Thing First: Go to the Website of your Architect Registration Board and Read all the Requirements of Obtaining an Architect License in your Jurisdiction
See the following link:
https://www.ncarb.org/get-licensed/state-licensing-boards

B. Download and Review the Latest ARE Documents at the NCARB Website

1. Important links to the FREE and official NCARB documents
NCARB launched ARE 5.0 on November 1, 2016. ARE 4.0 will continue to be available until June 30, 2018.

ARE candidates who started testing in ARE 4.0 can choose to "self-transition" to ARE 5.0. This will allow them to continue testing in the version that is most suitable for them. However, **once a candidate transitions to ARE 5.0, s/he cannot transition back to ARE 4.0**.

The current version of the Architect Registration Examination (ARE 5.0) includes six divisions:

- Practice Management (PcM)
- Project Management (PjM)
- Programming & Analysis (PA)
- Project Planning & Design (PPD)
- Project Development & Documentation (PDD)
- Construction & Evaluation (CE)

All ARE divisions continue to use **multiple choice, check-all-that-apply,** and **quantitative fill-in-the-blank**. The new exams include three new question types: **Hotspots, case studies,** and **drag-and-place**.

There is a tremendous amount of valuable information covering every step of becoming an architect available free of charge at the NCARB website:
http://www.ncarb.org/

For example, you can find guidance about architectural degree programs accredited by the National Architectural Accrediting Board (NAAB), NCARB's Architectural Experience Program (AXP) formerly known as Intern Development Program (IDP), and licensing requirements by state. These documents explain how you can qualify to take the Architect Registration Examination.

We find the official ARE 5.0 Guidelines, ARE 5.0 Handbook, and ARE 5.0 Credit Model extremely valuable. See the following link:
http://www.ncarb.org/ARE/ARE5.aspx

You should start by studying these documents.

2. **A detailed list and brief description of the FREE PDF files that you can download from NCARB**
   The following is a detailed list of the FREE PDF files that you can download from NCARB. They are listed in order based on their importance.

   - All **ARE 5.0** information can be found at the following links:
     http://www.ncarb.org/ARE/ARE5.aspx
     http://blog.ncarb.org/2016/November/ARE5-Study-Materials.aspx
   - The **ARE 5.0 Credit Model** is one of the most important documents, and tells you the easiest way to pass the ARE by taking selected divisions from ARE 4.0 and ARE 5.0.

ARE5.0:	Practice Management	Project Management	Programming & Analysis	Project Planning & Design	Project Development & Documentation	Construction & Evaluation
ARE 4.0:						
Construction Documents & Services	●	●			●	●
Programming Planning & Practice	●	●	●			
Site Planning & Design			●	●		
Building Design & Construction Systems				●	●	
Structural Systems				●	●	
Building Systems				●	●	
Schematic Design				●		

Figure 1.1 The relationship between ARE 4.0 and ARE 5.0

As shown in matrix above, if you are taking both ARE 4.0 and ARE 5.0, you can pass the ARE exams by taking only five divisions in total. To complete the ARE, your goal is to select and pass exams from both versions which cover all sixteen dots in matrix above. The quickest potential options are as follows:

a. You can take the following five divisions to pass the ARE:
ARE 4.0
- Construction Documents & Services
- Programming Planning & Practice
- Site Planning & Design

ARE 5.0
- Project Planning & Design
- Project Development & Documentation

OR

b. You can take the following five divisions to pass the ARE:
ARE 4.0
- Construction Documents & Services
- Programming Planning & Practice

ARE 5.0
- Programming & Analysis
- Project Planning & Design
- Project Development & Documentation

- **ARE 5.0 Guidelines** includes extremely valuable information on the ARE overview, NCARB, registration (licensure), architectural education requirements, the Architectural Experience Program (AXP), establishing your eligibility to test, scheduling an exam appointment, taking the ARE, receiving your score, retaking the ARE, the exam format, scheduling, and links to other FREE NCARB PDF files. You need to read this <u>at least twice</u>.

- **NCARB Education Guidelines** contains information on education requirements for initial licensure and for NCARB certification, satisfying the education requirement, foreign-educated applicants, the education alternative to NCARB certification, the Education Evaluation Services for Architects (EESA), the Education Standard, and other resources.

- **Architectural Experience Program (AXP) Guidelines** includes information on AXP overview, getting started and creating your NCARB record, experience areas and tasks, documenting your experience through hours, documenting your experience through a portfolio, and the next steps. You need to read this document <u>at least twice</u>. The information is valuable.

NCARB renamed the **Intern Development Program (IDP)** as **Architectural Experience Program (AXP)** in June 2016. Most of NCARB's 54-member boards have adopted the AXP as a prerequisite for initial architect licensure. Therefore, you should be familiar with the program.

The AXP application fee is $100. This fee includes one free transmittal of your Record for initial registration and keeps your Record active for the first year. After the initial year, there is an annual renewal fee required to maintain an active Record until you become registered. The cost is currently $85 each year. The fees are subject to change, and you need to check the NCARB website for the latest information.

There are two ways to meet the AXP requirements. The **first method** is **reporting hours**. Most candidates will use this method. You will need to document at least 3,740 required hours under the six different experience areas to complete the program. A minimum of 50% of your experience must be completed under the supervision of a qualified architect.

The following chart lists the hours required under the six experience areas:

Experience Area	Hours Required
Practice Management	160
Project Management	360
Programming & Analysis	260
Project Planning & Design	1,080
Project Development & Documentation	1,520
Construction & Evaluation	360
Total	**3,740**

Figure 1.2 The hours required under the six experience areas

Your experience reports will fall under one of **two experience settings**:
• **Setting A**: Work performed for an architecture firm.
• **Setting O**: Experiences performed outside an architecture firm.

You must earn at least **1,860 hours** in experience **setting A**.

Your AXP experience should be reported to NCARB at least every six months and logged within two months of completing each reporting period (the **Six-Month Rule**).

The **second method** to meet AXP requirements is to create an **AXP Portfolio**. This new method is for experienced design professionals who put their licensure on hold and allows you to prove your experience through the preparation of an online portfolio.

To complete the AXP through the **second method**, you will need to meet ALL the AXP criteria through the portfolio. In other words, you cannot complete the experience requirement through a combination of the **AXP portfolio** and **reporting hours**.

See the following link for more information on AXP:
https://www.ncarb.org/gain-axp-experience

• **Certification Guidelines** by NCARB (Skimming through this should be adequate. You should also forward a copy of this PDF file to your AXP supervisor.)

See the following link which contains resources for supervisors and mentors:
http://www.ncarb.org/Experience-Through-Internships/Supervisors-and-Mentors/Resources-for-Supervisor-and-Mentors.aspx

- **ARE 5.0 Related FAQs (Frequently Asked Questions)**: Skimming through this should be adequate.

- **Your Guide to ARE 5.0** includes information on understanding the basics of ARE 5.0, new question types, taking the test, making the transition, getting ARE 5.0 done, and planning your budget. The document also contains FAQs, and links for more information. You need to read this document <u>at least twice</u>. The information is valuable.

- **ARE 5.0 Handbook** contains an ARE overview, detailed information for each ARE division, and ARE 5.0 references. This handbook explains what NCARB expects you to know so that you can pass the ARE exams. ARE 5.0 uses either **Understand/Apply (U/A)** or **Analyze/Evaluate (A/E)** to designate the appropriate cognitive complexity of each objective, but *avoids* the use of **"Remember,"** the lowest level of cognitive complexity (CC), or **"Create,"** the highest level of CC.

  This handbook has some sample questions for each division. The real exam is like the samples in this handbook.

  Tips:
  - *ARE 5.0 Handbook has about 180 pages. To save time, you can just read the generic information at the front and back portion of the handbook, and focus on the ARE division(s) you are currently studying for. As you progress in your testing, you can read the applicable division that you are studying for. This way, the content will always be fresh in your mind.*
  - *You need to read this document <u>at least three times</u>. The information is valuable.*

- **ARE 5.0 Test Specification** identifies the ARE 5.0 division structure and defines the major content areas, called **Sections**; the measurement **Objectives**; and the percentage of content coverage, called **Weightings**. This document specifies the scope and objectives of each ARE division, and the percentage of questions in each content category. You need to read this document <u>at least twice</u>. The information is valuable, and is the base of all ARE exam questions.

- **ARE 5.0 Prep Videos** include one short video for each division. These videos give you a very good basic introduction to each division, including sample questions and answers, and explanations. You need to watch each video <u>at least three times</u>. See the following link:
  http://blog.ncarb.org/2016/November/ARE5-Study-Materials.aspx

- **The Burning Question: Why do we need an ARE anyway?** (We do not want to give out a link for this document because it is too long and keeps changing. You can Google it with its title. Skimming through this document should be adequate.)

- **Defining Your Moral Compass** (You can Google it with its title plus the word "NCARB." Skimming through this document should be adequate.)

- **Rules of Conduct** is available as a FREE PDF file at:
  http://www.ncarb.org/
  (Skimming through this should be adequate.)

C. The Intern Development Program (IDP)/Architectural Experience Program (AXP)

1. What is IDP? What is AXP?
IDP is a comprehensive training program jointly developed by the National Council of Architectural Registration Boards (NCARB) and the American Institute of Architects (AIA) to ensure that interns obtain the necessary skills and knowledge to practice architecture <u>independently</u>. NCARB renamed the **Intern Development Program (IDP)** as **Architectural Experience Program (AXP)** in June 2016.

2. Who qualifies as an intern?
Per NCARB, if an individual meets one of the following criteria, s/he qualifies as an intern:
a. Graduates from NAAB-accredited programs
b. Architecture students who acquire acceptable training prior to graduation
c. Other qualified individuals identified by a registration board

D. Overview of the Architect Registration Examination (ARE)

1. How to qualify for the ARE?
A candidate needs to qualify for the ARE via one of NCARB's member registration boards, or one of the Canadian provincial architectural associations.

Check with your Board of Architecture for specific requirements.

For example, in California, a candidate must provide verification of a minimum of <u>five</u> years of education and/or architectural work experience to qualify for the ARE.

Candidates can satisfy the five-year requirement in a variety of ways:

- Provide verification of a professional degree in architecture through a program that is accredited by NAAB or CACB.

  OR
- Provide verification of at least five years of educational equivalents.

  OR
- Provide proof of work experience under the direct supervision of a licensed architect.

See the following link:
http://www.ncarb.org/ARE/Getting-Started-With-the-ARE/Ready-to-Take-the-ARE-Early.aspx

2. **How to qualify for an architect license?**
    Again, each jurisdiction has its own requirements. An individual typically needs a combination of about <u>eight</u> years of education and experience, as well as passing scores on the ARE exams. See the following link:
    http://www.ncarb.org/Reg-Board-Requirements

    For example, the requirements to become a licensed architect in California are:
    *   Eight years of post-secondary education and/or work experience as evaluated by the Board (including at least one year of work experience under the direct supervision of an architect licensed in a U.S. jurisdiction or two years of work experience under the direct supervision of an architect registered in a Canadian province)
    *   Completion of the Architectural Experience Program (AXP)
    *   Successful completion of the Architect Registration Examination (ARE)
    *   Successful completion of the California Supplemental Examination (CSE)

    California does NOT require an accredited degree in architecture for examination and licensure. However, many other states do.

3. **What is the purpose of ARE?**
    The purpose of ARE is NOT to test a candidate's competency on every aspect of architectural practice. Its purpose is to test a candidate's competency on providing professional services to protect the <u>health, safety, and welfare</u> of the public. It tests candidates on the <u>fundamental</u> knowledge of pre-design, site design, building design, building systems, and construction documents and services.

    The ARE tests a candidate's competency as a "specialist" on architectural subjects. It also tests her abilities as a "generalist" to coordinate other consultants' works.

    You can download the exam content and references for each of the ARE divisions at the following links:
    https://www.ncarb.org/pass-the-are/start

4. **What is NCARB's rolling clock?**
    a. Starting on January 1, 2006, a candidate MUST pass ALL ARE sections within five years. A passing score for an ARE division is only valid for five years, and a candidate has to retake this division if she has NOT passed all divisions within the five-year period.

    b. Starting on January 1, 2011, a candidate who is authorized to take ARE exams MUST take at least one division of the ARE exams within five years of the authorization.

Otherwise, the candidate MUST apply for the authorization to take ARE exams from an NCARB member board again.

These rules were created by the **NCARB's rolling clock** resolution and passed by NCARB council during the 2004 NCARB Annual Meeting.

ARE 4.0 division expiration dates per the Rolling Clock will remain the same for the transition to ARE 5.0.

5. **How to register for an ARE exam?**
   See the instructions in the new ARE guideline at the following link:
   http://www.ncarb.org/ARE/ARE5.aspx

6. **How early do I need to arrive at the test center?**
   Be at the test center at least 30 minutes BEFORE your scheduled test time, OR you may lose your exam fee.

7. **Exam format & time**
   All ARE divisions are administered and graded by computer. The time allowances are as follows:

Division	Number of Questions	Test Duration	Appointment Time
Practice Management	80	2 hr 45 min	3 hr 30 min
Project Management	95	3 hr 15 min	4 hr
Programming & Analysis	95	3 hr 15 min	4 hr
Project Planning & Design	120	4 hr 15 min	5 hr
Project Development & Documentation	120	4 hr 15 min	5 hr
Construction & Evaluation	95	3 hr 15 min	4 hr
Total Time:		21 hr	25 hr 30 min

Figure 1.3   Exam format & time

Remote proctoring will be introduced mid December 2020. After December 13, 2020, the number of questions and time allotted will change to accommodate remote proctoring:

Division	Number of Questions	Test Duration	Appointment Time
Practice Management	65	2 hr 40 min	3 hr 20 min
Project Management	75	3 hr	3 hr 40 min
Programming & Analysis	75	3 hr	3 hr 40 min
Project Planning & Design	100	4 hr 5 min	5 hr
Project Development & Documentation	100	4 hr 5 min	5 hr
Construction & Evaluation	75	3 hr	3 hr 40 min
Total Time:		19 hr 50 min	24 hr 20 min

Figure 1.4   New Exam format & time

NCARB suggests you to arrive at the test center a minimum of 30 minutes before your scheduled appointment. You can have one flexible 15-minute break for each division. That is why the appointment time is 45 minutes longer than the actual test time for each division.

Practice Management has 80 questions and NCARB allows you 2 hours and 45 minutes to complete the exam, so you should spend an average of (2x60+45)/80=165/80= 2.06 minutes on each question.

Project Management and **Programming & Analysis** as well as **Construction & Evaluation** each have 95 questions and NCARB allows you 3 hours and 15 minutes to complete each exam, so you should spend an average of (3x60+15)/80=195/95= 2.05 minutes on each question.

Project Planning & Design as well as **Project Development & Documentation** each have 120 questions and NCARB allows you 4 hours and 15 minutes to complete each exam, so you should spend an average of (4x60+15)/120=255/120= 2.13 minutes on each question.

To simplify this, we suggest you spend about 2 minutes for each question in ALL divisions.

8. **How are ARE scores reported?**
   All ARE scores are reported as Pass or Fail. ARE scores are typically posted within 7 to 10 days. See the instructions in the new ARE guideline at the following link:
   http://www.ncarb.org/ARE/ARE5.aspx

9. **Is there a fixed percentage of candidates who pass the ARE exams?**
   No, there is NOT a fixed percentage of passing or failing. If you meet the minimum competency required to practice as an architect, you pass. The passing scores are the same for all Boards of Architecture.

10. **When can I retake a failed ARE division?**
    You can retake a failed division of the ARE 60 days after the previous attempt. You can only take the same ARE division three (3) times within any 12-month period.

11. **How much time do I need to prepare for each ARE division?**
    Every person is different, but on average you need about 40 to 80 hours to prepare for each ARE division. You need to set a realistic study schedule and stick with it. Make sure you allow time for personal and recreational commitments. If you are working full time, my suggestion is that you allow no less than 2 weeks but NOT more than 2 months to prepare for each ARE division. You should NOT drag out the exam prep process too long and risk losing your momentum.

12. **Which ARE division should I take first?**
    This is a matter of personal preference, and you should make the final decision.

Some people like to start with the easier divisions and pass them first. This way, they build more confidence as they study and pass each division.

Other people like to start with the more difficult divisions so that if they fail, they can keep busy studying and taking the other divisions while the clock is ticking. Before they know it, six months has passed and they can reschedule if need be.

13. ARE exam prep and test-taking tips

You can start with Construction & Evaluation (CE) because it gives a limited scope, and you may want to study building regulations and architectural history (especially famous architects and buildings that set the trends at critical turning points) before you take other divisions.

Complete mock exams and practice questions, including those provided by NCARB's practice program and this book, to hone your skills.

Form study groups and learn the exam experience of other ARE candidates. The forum at our website is a helpful resource. See the following links:
http://GreenExamEducation.com/
http://GeeForum.com/

Take the ARE exams as soon as you become eligible, since you probably still remember portions of what you learned in architectural school, especially structural and architectural history. Do not make excuses for yourself and put off the exams.

The following test-taking tips may help you:
* Pace yourself properly. You should spend about two minutes for each question on average.
* Read the questions carefully and pay attention to words like *best, could, not, always, never, seldom, may, false, except,* etc.
* For questions that you are not sure of, eliminate the obvious wrong answer and then make an educated guess. Please note that if you do NOT answer the question, you automatically lose the point. If you guess, you at least have a chance to get it right.
* If you have no idea what the correct answer is and cannot eliminate any obvious wrong answers, then do not waste too much time on the question and just guess. Try to use the same guess answer for all of the questions you have no idea about. For example, if you choose "d" as the guess answer, then you should be consistent and use "d" whenever you have no clue. This way, you are likely have a better chance at guessing more answers correctly.
* Mark the difficult questions, answer them, and come back to review them AFTER you finish all MC questions. If you are still not sure, go with your first choice. Your first choice is often the best choice.
* You really need to spend time practicing to become VERY familiar with NCARB's question types. This is because ARE is a timed test, and you do NOT have time to learn about the question types during the test. If you do not know them well, you will NOT be able to finish your solution on time.

- The ARE exams test a candidate's competency to provide professional services protecting the <u>health, safety, and welfare</u> of the public. Do NOT waste time on aesthetic or other design elements not required by the program.

ARE exams are difficult, but if you study hard and prepare well, combined with your experience, AXP training, and/or college education, you should be able to pass all divisions and eventually be able to call yourself an architect.

14. Strategies for passing ARE exams on the first try

Passing ARE exams on the first try, like everything else, needs not only hard work, but also great strategy.

- **Find out how much you already know and what you should study**
  You goal is NOT to read all the study materials. Your goal is to pass the exam. Flip through the study materials. If you already know the information, skip these parts.

  Complete the NCARB sample questions for the ARE exam you are preparing for NOW without ANY studying. See what percentage you get right. If you get 68% right, you should be able to pass the real exam without any studying. If you get 50% right, then you just need 18% more to pass.

  This "truth-finding" exam or exercise will also help you to find out what your weakness areas are, and what to focus on.

  Look at the same questions again at the end of your exam prep, and check the differences.

  Note: We suggest you study the sample questions in the official NCARB Study Guide first, and then other study materials, and then come back to NCARB sample questions again several days before the real ARE exam.

  Per NCARB, with the launch of the updated Architect Registration Examination (ARE) 5.0 in December 2020, the new cutting scores are based on the following information:

  "How Many Questions Do I Need Correct to Pass?

  Each division of the ARE measures different content knowledge areas. The difference in knowledge areas and the relative difficulty of the questions that make up that content area vary between divisions; therefore, expectations around how many questions you will need to answer correctly also changes from division to division.

  o **Project Development & Documentation and Construction & Evaluation**
    require the lowest percentage of scored items to be answered correctly to pass. You need to answer between **57 – 62 percent** of scored items correctly on these divisions to pass.

- o **Practice Management and Project Management** require a slightly higher percentage of questions to be answered correctly to pass. You need to answer between **62 – 68 percent** of scored items correctly on these divisions to pass.
- o **Programming & Analysis and Project Planning & Design** require the highest percentage of questions to be answered correctly to pass. You need to answer between **65 – 71 percent** of scored items correctly on these divisions to pass."

For detailed information, see the following link:
https://www.ncarb.org/blog/what-score-do-you-need-to-pass-the-are

- **Cherish and effectively use your limited time and effort**

  Let me paraphrase a story.
  One time someone had a chance to talk with Napoleon. He said:
  "You are such a great leader and have won so many battles, that you can use one of your soldiers to defeat ten enemy soldiers."

  Napoleon responded:
  "That may be true, but I always try to create opportunities where ten of my soldiers fight one enemy soldier. That is why I have won so many battles."

  Whether this story is true is irrelevant. The important thing that you need to know is **how to concentrate your limited time and effort to achieve your goal. Do NOT spread yourself too thin**. This is a principle many great leaders know and use and is why great leaders can use ordinary people to achieve extraordinary goals.

  Time and effort is the most valuable asset of a candidate. How to cherish and effectively use your limited time and effort is the key to passing any exam.

  If you study very hard and read many books, you are probably wasting your time. You are much better off picking one or two good books, covering the major framework of your exams, and then doing two sets of mock exams to find your weaknesses. You WILL pass if you follow this advice. You may still have minor weakness, but you will have covered your major bases.

- **Do NOT stretch your exam prep process too long**
  If you do this, it will hurt instead of help you. You may forget the information by the time you take the exam.

  Spend 40 to 80 hours for each division (a maximum of two months for the most difficult exams if you really need more time) should be enough. Once you decide on taking an exam, put in 100% of your effort and read the RIGHT materials. Allocate your time and effort on the most important materials, and you will pass.

- **Resist the temptation to read too many books and limit your time and effort to read only a few selected books or a few sections of each book in detail**

Having all the books but not reading them, or digesting ALL the information in them will not help you. It is like someone having a garage full of foods, and not eating or eating too much of them. Neither way will help.

You can only eat three meals a day. Similarly, you can ONLY absorb a certain amount of information during your exam prep. So, focus on the most important stuff.

Focus on your weaknesses but still read the other info. The key is to understand, digest the materials, and retain the information.

It is NOT how much you have read, but how much you understand, digest, and retain that counts.

The key to passing an ARE exam, or any other exam, is to know the scope of the exam, and not to read too many books. Select one or two really good books and focus on them. Actually <u>understand</u> the content and <u>memorize</u> it. For your convenience, I have <u>underlined</u> the fundamental information that I think is very important. You definitely need to <u>memorize</u> all the information that I have underlined.

You should try to understand the content first, and then memorize the content of the book by reading it multiple times. This is a much better way than relying on "mechanical" memory without understanding.

When you read the materials, ALWAYS keep the following in mind:

- **Think like an architect.**
  For example, when you take the Project Development & Documentation (PDD) exam, focus on what need to know to be able to coordinate your engineer's work, or tell them what to do. You are NOT taking an exam for becoming a structural engineer; you are taking an exam to become an architect.

  This criterion will help you filter out the materials that are irrelevant, and focus on the right information. You will know what to flip through, what to read line by line, and what to read multiple times.

  I have said this one thousand times, and I will say it once more:
  Time and effort is the most valuable asset of a candidate. How to cherish and effectively use your limited time and effort is the key to passing any exam.

15. ARE exam preparation requires short-term memory
You should understand that ARE Exam Preparation requires **Short-Term Memory**. This is especially true for the MC portion of the exam. You should schedule your time accordingly: in the <u>early</u> stages of your ARE exam Preparation, you should focus on <u>understanding</u> and an **<u>initial</u>** review of the material; in the <u>late</u> stages of your exam preparation, you should focus on <u>memorizing</u> the material as a **<u>final</u>** review.

16. Allocation of your time and scheduling

You should spend about 60% of your effort on the most important and fundamental study materials, about 30% of your effort on mock exams, and the remaining 10% on improving your weakest areas, i.e., reading and reviewing the questions that you answered incorrectly, reinforcing the portions that you have a hard time memorizing, etc.

Do NOT spend too much time looking for <u>obscure</u> ARE information because the NCARB will HAVE to test you on the most **common** architectural knowledge and information. At least <u>80% to 90%</u> of the exam content will have to be the most <u>common</u>, <u>important</u> and <u>fundamental</u> knowledge. The exam writers can word their questions to be <u>tricky</u> or <u>confusing</u>, but they have to limit themselves to the <u>important</u> content; otherwise, their tests will NOT be legally defensible. At most, <u>10%</u> of their test content can be <u>obscure</u> information. You only need to answer about 68% of all the questions. So, if you master the common ARE knowledge (applicable to 90% of the questions) and use the guess technique for the remaining 10% of the questions on the obscure ARE content, you will do well and pass the exam.

On the other hand, if you focus on the obscure ARE knowledge, you may answer the entire 10% <u>obscure</u> portion of the exam correctly, but only answer half of the remaining 90% of the <u>common</u> ARE knowledge questions correctly, and you will fail the exam. That is why we have seen many smart people who can answer very difficult ARE questions correctly because they are able to look them up and do quality research. However, they often end up failing ARE exams because they cannot memorize the common ARE knowledge needed on the day of the exam. ARE exams are NOT an open-book exams, and you cannot look up information during the exam.

The **process of memorization** is like **filling a cup with a hole at the bottom**: You need to fill it <u>faster</u> than the water leaks out at the bottom, and you need to <u>constantly</u> fill it; otherwise, it will quickly be empty.

Once you memorize something, your brain has already started the process of forgetting it. It is natural. That is how we have enough space left in our brain to remember the really important things.

It is tough to fight against your brain's natural tendency to forget things. Acknowledging this truth and the fact that you can<u>not</u> memorize everything you read, you need to <u>focus</u> your limited time, energy and brainpower on the <u>most important</u> issues.

The biggest danger for most people is that they memorize the information in the early stages of their exam preparation, but forget it before or on the day of the exam and still THINK they remember them.

Most people fail the exam NOT because they cannot answer the few "advanced" questions on the exam, but because they have read the information but can <u>NOT</u> recall it on the day of the exam. They spend too much time preparing for the exam, drag the preparation process on too long, seek too much information, go to too many websites, do too many practice questions and too many mock exams (one or two sets of mock exams can be good for you), and **spread themselves too thin**. They end up **missing the most important information** of the exam, and they will fail.

The ARE Mock Exam series along with the tips and methodology in each of the books will help you find and improvement your weakness areas, MEMORIZE the most important aspects of the test to pass the exam ON THE FIRST TRY.

So, if you have a lot of time to prepare for the ARE exams, you should plan your effort accordingly. You want your ARE knowledge to peak at the time of the exam, not before or after.

For example, <u>if you have two months to prepare for a very difficult ARE exam</u>, you may want to spend the first month focused on <u>reading and understanding</u> all of the study materials you can find as your **initial** review. Also during this first month, you can start <u>memorizing</u> after you understand the materials as long as you know you HAVE to review the materials again later to <u>retain</u> them. If you have memorized something once, it is easier to memorize it again later.

Next, you can spend two weeks focused on <u>memorizing</u> the material. You need to review the material at least three times. You can then spend one week on <u>mock exams</u>. The last week before the exam, focus on retaining your knowledge and reinforcing your weakest areas. Read the mistakes that you have made and think about how to avoid them during the real exam. Set aside a mock exam that you <u>have not taken</u> and take it seven days before test day. This will alert you to your weaknesses and provide direction for the remainder of your studies.

<u>If you have one week to prepare for the exam</u>, you can spend two days reading and understanding the study material, two days repeating and memorizing the material, two days on mock exams, and one day retaining the knowledge and enforcing your weakest areas.

The last one to two weeks before an exam is <u>absolutely</u> critical. You need to have the "do or die" mentality and be ready to study hard to pass the exam on your first try. That is how some people are able to pass an ARE exam with only one week of preparation.

17. Timing of review: the 3016 rule; memorization methods, tips, suggestions, and mnemonics

Another important strategy is to review the material in a timely manner. Some people say that the best time to <u>review</u> material is between <u>30 minutes and 16 hours</u> (the **3016** rule) after you read it for the first time. So, if you review the material right after you read it for the first time, the review may not be helpful.

I have personally found this method extremely beneficial. The best way for me to memorize study materials is to review what I learned during the day again in the evening. This, of course, happens to fall within the timing range mentioned above.

Now that you know the **3016** rule, you may want to schedule your review accordingly. For example, you may want to read <u>new</u> study materials in the morning and afternoon, then after dinner do an <u>initial review</u> of what you learned during the day.

OR

If you are working full time, you can read <u>new</u> study materials in the evening or at night and then get up early the next morning to spend one or two hours on an <u>initial review</u> of what you learned the night before.

The <u>initial</u> review and memorization will make your <u>final</u> review and memorization much easier.

Mnemonics is a very good way for you to memorize facts and data that are otherwise very hard to memorize. It is often <u>arbitrary</u> or <u>illogical</u> but it works.

A good mnemonic can help you remember something for a long time or even a lifetime after reading it just once. Without the mnemonics, you may read the same thing many times and still not be able to memorize it.

There are a few common Mnemonics:
1) **Visual** Mnemonics: Link what you want to memorize to a visual image.
2) **Spatial** Mnemonics: link what you want to memorize to a space, and the order of things in it.
3) **Group** Mnemonics: <u>Break up</u> a difficult piece <u>into</u> several smaller and more <u>manageable groups or sets</u>, and memorize the sets and their order. One example is the grouping of the 10-digit phone number into three groups in the U.S. This makes the number much easier to memorize.
4) **Architectural** Mnemonics: A combination of <u>Visual</u> Mnemonics and <u>Spatial</u> Mnemonics and <u>Group</u> Mnemonics.

Imagine you are walking through a building several times, along the same path. You should be able to remember the order of each room. You can then break up the information that you want to remember and link them to several images, and then imagine you hang the images on walls of various rooms. You should be able to easily recall each group in an orderly manner by imagining you are walking through the building again on the same path, and looking at the images hanging on walls of each room. When you look at the images on the wall, you can easily recall the related information.

You can use your home, office or another building that you are <u>familiar with</u> to build an <u>Architectural</u> Mnemonics to help you to organize the things you need to memorize.

5) **Association** Mnemonics: You can <u>associate</u> what you want to memorize <u>with a sentence</u>, a similarly pronounced word, or a place you are familiar with, etc.
6) **Emotion** Mnemonics: Use emotion to fix an image in your memory.
7) **First Letter** Mnemonics: You can use the <u>first letter</u> of what you want to memorize <u>to construct a sentence or acronym</u>. For example, "**Roy G. Biv**" can be used to memorize

the order of the 7 colors of the rainbow, it is composed of the first letter of each primary color.

You can use **<u>Association</u>** Mnemonics and memorize them as <u>all</u> the plumbing fixtures for a typical home, PLUS Urinal.

OR
You can use "Water S K U L" (**<u>First Letter</u>** Mnemonics selected from website below) to memorize them:

<u>Water </u>Closets
<u>S</u>hower
<u>K</u>itchen Sinks
<u>U</u>rinal
<u>L</u>avatory

18. The importance of good and effective study methods

There is a saying: Give a man a fish, feed him for a day. Teach a man to fish, feed him for a lifetime. I think there is some truth to this. Similarly, it is better to teach someone HOW to study than just give him good study materials. In this book, I give you good study materials to save you time, but more importantly, I want to teach you effective study methods so that you can not only study and pass ARE exams, but also so that you will benefit throughout the rest of your life for anything else you need to study or achieve. For example, I give you samples of mnemonics, but I also teach you the more important thing: HOW to make mnemonics.

Often in the same class, all the students study almost the SAME materials, but there are some students that always manage to stay at the top of the class and get good grades on exams. Why? One very important factor is they have good study methods.

Hard work is important, but it needs to be combined with effective study methods. I think people need to work hard AND work SMART to be successful at their work, career, or anything else they are pursuing.

19. The importance of repetition: read this book <u>at least</u> three times

Repetition is one of the most important tips for learning. That is why I have listed it under a separate title. For example, you should treat this book as part of the core study materials for your ARE exams and you need to read this book <u>at least three times</u> to get all of its benefits:

1) The first time you read it, it is new information. You should focus on understanding and digesting the materials, and also do an <u>initial</u> review with the **3016** rule.
2) The second time you read it, focus on reading the parts <u>I</u> have already highlighted AND <u>you</u> have <u>highlighted</u> (the important parts and the weakest parts for you).
3) The third time, focus on <u>memorizing</u> the information.

Remember the analogy of the <u>memorization process</u> as **filling a cup with a hole on the bottom**?
Do NOT stop reading this book until you pass the real exam.

20. The importance of a routine

A routine is very important for studying. You should try to set up a routine that works for you. First, look at how much time you have to prepare for the exam, and then adjust your current routine to include exam preparation. Once you set up the routine, stick with it.

For example, you can spend from 8:00 a.m. to 12:00 noon, and 1:00 p.m. to 5:00 p.m. on studying new materials, and 7:00 p.m. to 10:00 p.m. to do an initial review of what you learned during the daytime. Then, switch your study content to mock exams, memorization and retention when it gets close to the exam date. This way, you have 11 hours for exam preparation everyday. You can probably pass an ARE exam in one week with this method. Just keep repeating it as a way to <u>retain</u> the architectural knowledge.

OR
You can spend 7:00 p.m. to 10:00 p.m. on studying new materials, and 6:00 a.m. to 7:00 a.m. to do an initial review of what you learned the evening before. This way, you have four hours for exam preparation every day. You can probably pass an ARE exam in two weeks with this preparation schedule.

A routine can help you to memorize important information because it makes it easier for you to concentrate and work with your body clock.

Do NOT become panicked and change your routine as the exam date gets closer. It will not help to change your routine and pull all-nighters right before the exam. In fact, if you pull an all-nighter the night before the exam, you may do much worse than you would have done if you kept your routine.

All-nighters or staying up late are not effective. For example, if you break your routine and stay up one-hour late, you will feel tired the next day. You may even have to sleep a few more hours the next day, adversely affecting your study regimen.

21. The importance of short, frequent breaks and physical exercise

Short, frequent breaks and physical exercise are VERY important for you, especially when you are spending a lot of time studying. They help relax your body and mind, making it much easier for you to concentrate when you study. They make you more efficient.

Take a five-minute break, such as a walk, at least once every one to two hours. Do at least 30 minutes of physical exercise every day.

If you feel tired and cannot concentrate, stop, go outside, and take a five-minute walk. You will feel much better when you come back.

You need your body and brain to work well to be effective with your studying. Take good care of them. You need them to be well-maintained and in excellent condition. You need to be able to count on them when you need them.

If you do not feel like studying, maybe you can start a little bit on your studies. Just casually read a few pages. Very soon, your body and mind will warm up and you will get into study mode.

Find a room where you will NOT be disturbed when you study. A good study environment is essential for concentration.

22. A strong vision and a clear goal

You need to have a strong vision and a clear goal: to <u>master</u> the architectural knowledge and <u>become an architect in the shortest time</u>. This is your number one priority. You need to master the architectural knowledge BEFORE you do sample questions or mock exams, except "truth-finding" exam or exercise at the very beginning of your exam prep. It will make the process much easier. Everything we discuss is to help you achieve this goal.

As I have mentioned on many occasions, and I say it one more time here because it is so important:

It is how much architectural knowledge and information you can <u>understand, digest, memorize</u>, and firmly retain that matters, not how many books you read or how many sample tests you have taken. The books and sample tests will NOT help you if you cannot understand, digest, memorize, and retain the important information for the ARE exam.

Cherish your limited <u>time and effort</u> and focus on the most <u>important</u> information.

23. Codes and standards used in this book

We use the following codes and standards:
American Institute of Architects, Contract Documents, Washington, DC; ADA Standards for Accessible Design, ADA; Various International Codes by ICC. See Appendixes for more information.

24. Where can I find study materials on architectural history?

Every ARE exam may have a few questions related to architectural history. The following are some helpful links to FREE study materials on the topic:
http://issuu.com/motimar/docs/history_synopsis?viewMode=magazine

Chapter Two

Project Management (PjM) Division

A. General Information

1. Exam content

The PjM division of the ARE has 95 questions which cover five different areas.

Sections	Target Percentage	Expected Number of Items
Section 1: Resource Management	7-13%	6-12
Section 2: Project Work Planning	17-23%	16-22
Section 3: Contracts	25-31%	23-29
Section 4: Project Execution	17-23%	16-22
Section 5: Project Quality Control	19-25%	18-23

Figure 2.1   Exam format & time

Note:
After December 13, 2020, the number of questions will be reduced. See Figure 1.4.

The exam content can be further broken down as follows:
Section 1: Resource Management (7-13%)
- Determine criteria required to assemble team
- Assess criteria required to allocate and manage project resources (A/E)

Section 2: Project Work Planning (17-23%)
- Develop and maintain project work plan (U/A)
- Determine criteria required to develop and maintain project schedule (A/E)
- Determine appropriate communication to project team – owner, contractor, consultants and internal staff (U/A)

Section 3: Contracts (25-31%)
- Evaluate and verify adherence to owner/architect agreement (A/E)
- Interpret key elements of, and verify adherence to architect/consultant agreement (U/A)
- Interpret key elements of the owner/contractor agreement (U/A)
- Interpret key elements of the owner/consultant agreement to integrate the consultant's work into the project (U/A)

Section 4: Project Execution (17-23%)
- Evaluate compliance with construction budget (A/E)
- Evaluate and address changes in scope of work and scope creep (A/E)
- Evaluate project documentation to ensure it supports the specified delivery method (A/E)
- Identify and conform with the requirements set forth by authorities having jurisdiction in order to obtain approvals for the project (U/A)

Section 5: Project Quality Control (19-25%)
- Apply procedures required for adherence to laws and regulations relating to the project (U/A)
- Identify steps in maintaining project quality control, and reducing risks and liabilities (A/E)
- Perform quality control reviews of project documentation throughout life of project (A/E)
- Evaluate management of the design process to maintain integrity of design objectives (A/E)

2. **Official exam guide and reference index for the Project Management (PjM) division**

NCARB published the exam guides for all ARE 5.0 division together as *ARE 5.0 Handbook*.

You need to read the official exam guide for the PPD division at least three times and become very familiar with it. The real exam is VERY similar to the sample questions in the handbook.

You can download the official *ARE 5.0 Handbook* at the following link:
https://www.ncarb.org/sites/default/files/ARE5-Handbook.pdf

Note: We suggest you study the official ARE 5.0 Handbook first, and then other study materials, and then come back to Handbook again several days before the real ARE exam.

B. **The Most Important Documents/Publications for Project Management (PjM) Division of the ARE Exam**

1. **Official NCARB list of references for the Project Management (PjM) division with our comments and suggestions**
   You can find the NCARB list of references for this division in the Appendixes of this book and the *ARE 5.0 Handbook*.

Note:
*While many of the MC questions in the real ARE exam **focus on design concepts**, there are **some questions requiring calculations**.*

In the ARE exams, it may be a good idea to skip any calculation question that requires over 2 minutes of your time; just pick a guess answer, mark it, and come back to calculate it at the end. This way, you have more time to read and answer other easier questions correctly.

A calculation question that takes 20 minutes to answer will gain the same number of points as a simple question that ONLY takes 2 minutes.

If you spend 20 minutes on a calculation question earlier, you risk losing the time to read and answer ten other easier questions, which could result in a loss of ten points instead of one.

The following is the NCARB list of top references for this division. For a longer list of relevant reference materials, please see the reference matrix at the end of this book.

Publications
The Architect's Handbook of Professional Practice
The American Institute of Architects
John Wiley & Sons, 14th edition (2008) and 15th edition (2014)

Professional Practice: A Guide to Turning Designs into Buildings
Paul Segal, FAIA
W. W. Norton, 2006

AIA Contract Documents
The following list of AIA Contract Documents have content covered in the Project Management division.

A101-2017
Standard Form of Agreement Between Owner and Contractor where the basis of payment is a Stipulated Sum

A133-2019
Standard Form of Agreement Between Owner and Construction Manager as Constructor where the basis of payment is the Cost of the Work Plus a Fee with a Guaranteed Maximum Price

A195-2008
Standard Form of Agreement Between Owner and Contractor for Integrated Project Delivery

A201-2017
General Conditions of the Contract for Construction

A295-2008
General Conditions of the Contract for Integrated Project Delivery

B101-2017
Standard Form of Agreement Between Owner and Architect

B195-2008
Standard Form of Agreement Between Owner and Architect for Integrated Project Delivery

C401-2017
Standard Form of Agreement Between Architect and Consultant

The following are some extra study materials that are useful if you have some additional time and want to learn more. If you are tight on time, you can simply look through them and focus on the sections that cover your weaknesses:

2. **Construction Specifications Institute (CSI) MasterFormat &** *Building Construction*
Become familiar with the new 6-digit CSI Construction Specifications Institute (CSI) MasterFormat as there may be a few questions based on this publication. Make sure you know which items/materials belong to which CSI MasterFormat specification section, and memorize the major section names and related numbers. For example, Division 9 is Finishes, and Division 5 is Metal, etc. Another one of my books, *Building Construction*, has detailed discussions on CSI MasterFormat specification sections.

Mnemonics for the 2004 CSI MasterFormat

The following is a good mnemonic, which relates to the 2004 CSI MasterFormat division names. Bold font signals the gaps in the numbering sequence.

This tool can save you lots of time: if you can remember the four sentences below, you can easily memorize the order of the 2004 CSI MasterFormat divisions. The number sequencing is a bit more difficult, but can be mastered if you remember the five bold words and numbers that are not sequential. Memorizing this material will not only help you in several divisions of the ARE, but also in real architectural practice

Mnemonics (pay attention to the underlined letters):
Good students can memorize material when teachers order.
F students earn F's simply 'cause **forgetting** principles have **an** effect. (21 and 25)
C students **end** everyday understanding things without memorizing. (31)
Please make professional pollution prevention inventions **everyday**. (40 and 48)

1-Good.................................. General Requirements
2-Students............................. (Site) now Existing Conditions
3-Can.................................... Concrete
4-Memorize............................ Masonry
5-Material .... Metals
6-When.................................. Woods and Plastics

7-<u>T</u>eachers.............................<u>T</u>hermal and Moisture
8-<u>O</u>rder..................................<u>O</u>penings

9-<u>F</u>..<u>F</u>inishes
10-<u>S</u>tudents............................<u>S</u>pecialties
11-<u>E</u>arn..................................<u>E</u>quipment
12-<u>F</u>'s....................................<u>F</u>urnishings
13-<u>S</u>imply..............................<u>S</u>pecial Construction
14-'<u>C</u>ause...............................<u>C</u>onveying
21-<u>F</u>orgetting .... <u>F</u>ire
22-<u>P</u>rinciples..........................<u>P</u>lumbing
23-<u>H</u>ave................................ <u>H</u>VAC
25-<u>A</u>n..................................... <u>A</u>utomation
26-<u>E</u>ffect.............................. <u>E</u>lectric

27-<u>C</u>..<u>C</u>ommunication
28-<u>S</u>tudents............................ <u>S</u>afety & Security
31-<u>E</u>nd.................................... <u>E</u>arthwork
32-<u>E</u>veryday...........................<u>E</u>xterior
33-<u>U</u>nderstanding ....<u>U</u>tilities
34-<u>T</u>hings...............................<u>T</u>ransportation
35-<u>W</u>ithout <u>M</u>emorizing........ <u>W</u>aterways and <u>M</u>arine

40-<u>P</u>lease...............................<u>P</u>rocess Integration
41-<u>M</u>ake................................. <u>M</u>aterial Processing and Handling Equipment
42-<u>P</u>rofessional..................... <u>P</u>rocess Heating, Cooling, and Drying Equipment
43-<u>P</u>ollution.......................... <u>P</u>rocess Gas and Liquid Handling, Purification and Storage Equipment
44-<u>P</u>revention........................<u>P</u>ollution Control Equipment
45-<u>I</u>nventions........................ <u>I</u>ndustry-Specific Manufacturing Equipment
48-<u>E</u>veryday..........................<u>E</u>lectrical Power Generation

Note:
There are 49 CSI divisions. The "missing" divisions are those "reserved for future expansion" by CSI. They are intentionally omitted from the list.

Chapter Three

ARE Mock Exam for
Project Management (PjM) Division

A. Multiple-Choice (MC)

1. Two construction firms are working on the same building with one owner. One firm is working with the owner on the building shell, and the other is working with the owner on the interior improvement under a separate contract. This arrangement is known as
   a. a multiple prime
   b. an associated firm
   c. a joint venture
   d. partnering

2. A homeowner asks an architect's opinion on whether to renovate his home or to completely demolish it and build a new one. The architect should suggest the homeowner to:
   a. compare the cost of the two choices
   b. seek LEED certification for the home
   c. complete a feasibility study
   d. complete a life safety study

3. Blocking and stacking are
   a. terms used in masonry construction
   b. terms used in programming
   c. terms used in structural calculations
   d. terms used in design development

4. What does the first C in CC&R stand for?
   a. Conditions
   b. Covenants
   c. Cost
   d. Codes

5. Which of the following can cause mold inside a building wall? **Check the three that apply.**
   a. poor ventilation
   b. poor drainage
   c. flashing
   d. organic feedstock
   e. EIFS

6. An architectural project program should include which of the following? **Check the four that apply.**
   a. a basis of design
   b. owner project requirements
   c. type of structural system
   d. type of HVAC system
   e. a budget
   f. type and quantity of spaces

7. The project schedule in figure 3.1 on the following page is known as a
   a. Gantt chart
   b. critical path method (CPM)
   c. program evaluation and review technique (PERT)
   d. project cycle method (PCM)

8. What is the total numbers of days needed to finish the project per the project schedule in figure 3.1?
   a. 24
   b. 32
   c. 36
   d. 38

9. The dashed arrows in figure 3.1 are known as
   a. knots
   b. paths
   c. dummies
   d. processes

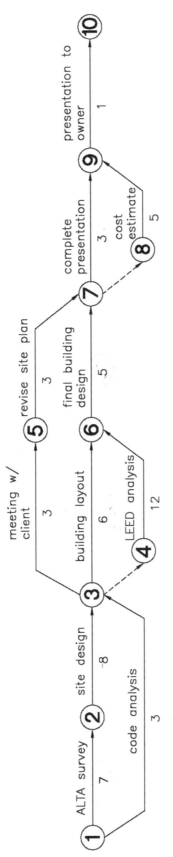

Figure 3.1 Project Schedule

10. After the award of a construction contract, which of the following shall the contractor submit for architect review?
    a. a punch list
    b. a schedule of construction
    c. a list of potential change orders
    d. a change order log
    e. a submittal log

11. Which of the following types of estimates is the most accurate?
    a. unit price
    b. an estimate based on the construction cost of similar buildings
    c. cost of building systems
    d. historical data of the same type of construction

12. An owner wants the architect to transfer ownership of the architectural plans and specifications to the owner as a prerequisite to granting the design contract. What is the best solution if the architect wants to get the job while still protecting the interests of her firm? **Check the two that apply.**
    a. Tell the owner that the architect should have copyrights of all documents generated by the architect per the AIA documents.
    b. Transfer ownership of the architect's plans and specifications to the owner and require the owner to sign a waiver releasing the architect of the liabilities for unauthorized use of the documents.
    c. Negotiate with the owner and try to seek joint-ownership of the plans and specifications.
    d. Refuse the owner's request.

13. Which of the following is characteristic of a fast-track project? **Check the two that apply.**
    a. The design phase occurs before the construction phase.
    b. The design phase overlaps the construction phase.
    c. Multiple bid packages are involved.
    d. One bid package is utilized to simplify the construction process.

14. Which of the following is the most important consideration in an architect/owner contract? **Check the two that apply.**
    a. scope of services
    b. consultants
    c. type of construction
    d. architectural service fees

15. Which of the following is typically not required for a new library building plan check?
    a. a planning department plan check fee
    b. a building department plan check fee
    c. a fire department plan check fee
    d. a health department plan check fee
    e. a school district fee
    f. a drainage fee

16. The cost for a geotechnical survey is typically borne by the
    a. owner
    b. architect
    c. contractor
    d. federal government

17. The best way to reduce the number of change orders is to
    a. hold regular coordination meetings
    b. use an outside peer review service
    c. issue multiple bid packages
    d. have owners review the plans
    e. finish coordination and quality control before issuing the bid package

18. Which of the following is an effective way to improve the quality of construction documents? **Check the two that apply.**
    a. communication among employees
    b. hiring qualified employees
    c. having owners review the plans
    d. using outside consultants

19. AIA Document C401-2007 includes a new flow-down provision to extend the responsibilities and rights between which of the following parties?
    a. the owner and the contractor
    b. the architect and the owner
    c. the architect and the contractor
    d. none of the above

20. Outline specifications during the schematic design stage are typically broken down by
    a. divisions
    b. disciplines
    c. costs
    d. the critical path method

21. Bid alternates to choose between stone veneer and brick veneer, double-glazing and single-glazing, and clay roof tiles and asphalt shingles are most likely the architect's attempt to
    a. incorporate environmental friendly options
    b. control construction costs
    c. anticipate HOA CC&R requirements
    d. address neighborhood concerns

22. A specific plan is typically developed or paid for by the?
    a. city
    b. civil engineer
    c. architect
    d. structural engineer
    e. owner
    f. contractor

23. An EIR is typically paid for by the?
    a. city
    b. civil engineer
    c. architect
    d. structural engineer
    e. owner
    f. contractor

24. During the construction documents phase of work, the architect receives the plan check corrections. Which of the following is the most effective way to coordinate the engineering consultant's work?
    a. Send the entire plan check corrections list to all the consultants, and then start to review the plan check corrections list.
    b. Review the plan check corrections list first, and then send only the relevant part of the plan check corrections list to the related consultants.
    c. Review and mark up the plan check corrections, mark up the consultants' plans per the list, and then send only the relevant part of the plan check corrections list and the marked-up sheets of the consultants' plans to the related consultants.
    d. Review and mark up the plan check corrections, mark up the consultants' plans per the list, and then send only the relevant part of the plan check corrections list and entire set of the consultants' plans with the mark-ups to the related consultants.

25. Which of the following is true according to A101–2007, Standard Form of Agreement Between Owner and Contractor where the basis of payment is a Stipulated Sum? **Check the two that apply.**
    a. Mediation is binding in most states.
    b. Arbitration is binding in most states.
    c. Mediation is mandatory.
    d. Arbitration is submitted to AIA.

26. Governing agencies regulate the development of projects through which of the following? **Check the two that apply.**
    a. General plans
    b. Specific plans
    c. CC&R
    d. plumbing permits

27. Which of the following will affect a project's schedule? **Check the three that apply.**
    a. the client
    b. the number of project team members
    c. the architect
    d. insurance

28. Which of the following will restrict a project's development? **Check the three that apply.**
    a. the municipal codes
    b. the building codes
    c. the experience of construction workers
    d. the fire department

29. Which of the following does a soils report typically include? **Check the two that apply.**
    a. landscaping
    b. seismic considerations
    c. utilities
    d. footing and foundation design guidelines

30. Which of the following is the correct order of arranging the units used in the Public Land Survey System (PLSS) in the US, from large to small?
    a. check, section, township
    b. section, township, check
    c. check, township, section
    d. section, check, township

31. Which of the following is a measure to improve water quality? **Check the two that apply.**
    a. retention pond
    b. detention pond
    c. concrete swale
    d. trench drain

32. Which of the following is the best method to reduce asbestos exposure in an existing building?
    a. Remove the asbestos.
    b. Keep asbestos-containing materials in place without disturbing it.
    c. Seal off the spaces with asbestos-containing materials.
    d. Ban children from rooms with asbestos containing materials.

33. Which of the following does not regulate a building's height?
    a. zoning codes
    b. building codes
    c. CC&R
    d. ADA

34. Which of the following do not need to comply with ADA Accessibility Guidelines (ADAAG)?
    a. a city hall building

b. a single-family home on a private property
c. a construction trailer
d. both b & c

35. In a construction project, a contractor's insurance will pay for claims from the owner, if the owner waives his rights to sue for and recover from the contractor. This arrangement is an example of (**Check the two that apply.**)
a. a waiver of subrogation
b. an exclusive right
c. an exculpatory clause
d. a waiver of abrogation

36. Per AIA Document B101-2007, which of the following regarding mediation is true? **Check the two that apply.**
a. Mediation shall always precede litigation.
b. The prevailing party will be reimbursed for the mediation fees.
c. Arbitration shall always precede mediation.
d. The parties shall share the mediation fees equally.

37. Which of the following can use eminent domain to acquire land for the project development? **Check the two that apply.**
a. a public school
b. a toll road
c. an interstate freeway
d. a shopping center

38. Which of the following project types receives the most tax incentive with regard to historical buildings?
a. preservation
b. rehabilitation
c. restoration
d. reconstruction

39. Which of the following is the correct order to arrange building types based on their building efficiencies, from high to low?
a. department store, office, apartment, hospital
b. department store, apartment, office, hospital
c. office, apartment, hospital, department store
d. office, apartment, department store, hospital

40. Which of the following are not considered laws?
a. USGBC LEED reference guides
b. building codes
c. ADA
d. municipal codes
e. EPA Codes of Federal Regulations

41. Which of the following can reduce stormwater runoff and alleviate the urban heat island effect? **Check the three that apply.**
    a. increasing the site coverage ratio
    b. increasing Floor Area Ratio (FAR)
    c. using a vegetated roof
    d. using porous pavement with high albedo
    e. building a retention pond on the site

42. Recycled materials will contribute to which of the following?
    a. traffic alleviation and smog reduction
    b. protection of virgin materials
    c. energy savings
    d. MEP cost savings

43. According to the USGBC, which of the following is not graywater?
    a. water from kitchen sinks
    b. water from toilet
    c. harvest rainwater
    d. water from outdoor area drains
    e. none of above
    f. a, b, c, and d

44. Which of the following is not true? **Check the two that apply.**
    a. Water from kitchen sinks can be reused for landscape irrigation or flushing toilets.
    b. Water from kitchen sinks cannot be reused for landscape irrigation or flushing toilets.
    c. Reclaimed water requires special piping with a different color.
    d. Reclaimed water cannot reduce potable water use.

45. A LEED certified building has the following extra costs when compared with a conventional building?
    a. hard costs
    b. soft costs
    c. storm control costs
    d. life cycle analysis costs
    e. life cycle cost analysis

46. All LEED rating systems include credits for:
    a. emission measurement.
    b. radon alleviation.
    c. minimum energy performance.
    d. innovation.

47. Which of the following have the lowest ODP?
    a. CFCs
    b. HCFCs

    c. HFCs

    d. This is hard to determine.

48. Choose the post-consumer item from the following.
    a. construction debris sent to a recycle facility
    b. scraps from a manufacturing process
    c. books from a print overrun
    d. scraps from a manufacturing process that were reclaimed and used in a different manufacturing process

49. Which of the following evaluates the environmental performance of services and products?
    a. ASTM
    b. ISO 14000
    c. ANSI
    d. LEED

50. An architect has a total design budget of $210,000 for a supermarket. The design schedule is 8 weeks long at 40 hours per week. 35% of the design fee is allocated to the design consultants. The firm intends to achieve a 3.0 multiplier for all employees. 20% of the principal's time will be allocated to this project. Utilization of the Project Architect, Job Captain, and Drafter should be maximized. Drag the numbers from the left to the proper box to finish the labor schedule. Not all numbers will be used while some numbers can be used more than once.

8	Available staff	Direct Rate	Weekly person-hour
20.95	Principal	$105	
22.95	Project Manager	$50	
24.95	Project Architect	$40	
30	Job Captain	$30	
40	Drafter	$20	

Figure 3.2   Labor Schedule

51. Which of the following statements regarding the design-build approach are true? **Check the three that apply.**
    a. It has been used for more than 4,000 years.
    b. It is a new approach developed in the nineteenth century.
    c. If an architect is leading a design-build project, she needs to be responsible for the accuracy of her consultant's work.
    d. If an architect is leading a design-build project, she needs to coordinate, but will not be responsible for the accuracy of her consultant's work.
    e. If an architect is leading design-build project, she needs to schedule and control the

means and methods of construction.

    f.   If an architect is leading a design-build project, she needs to coordinate, but the contractor will schedule and control the means and methods of construction.

52. In reference to bridged design-build, which of the following statements are correct?
    a.   Bridged design-build is just another name for design-build.
    b.   A contractor is acting as a bridge between the architect and the owner.
    c.   An architect is acting as a bridge between the contractor and the owner.
    d.   The owner eventually hires two architects.

53. In the construction documents phase, the owner requests changes that will delay bidding by three weeks, delay permitting by four weeks, and add two weeks to the construction schedule.

Drag and drop the project completion point in the schedule below to a new location which reflects the impact of these changes. Each vertical column on the schedule represents one week.

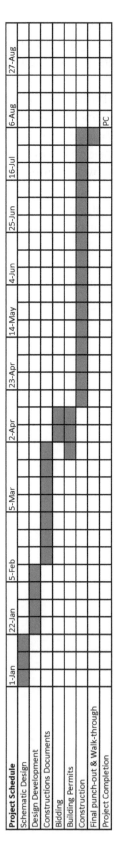

Figure 3.3   Project Schedule

54. A new mechanical system is required to make a historic building functional. Which of the following is recommended?
    a. Place the mechanical unit in the attic and remove a substantial amount of building materials.
    b. Place the mechanical unit in an existing masonry unit enclosure and cut through the existing masonry walls.
    c. Place the mechanical unit on the ground and enclose it with hedges.
    d. Place the mechanical unit on the roof top and add additional beams and columns to support the unit

55. Which of the following procedure is recommended for historic building?
    a. Identifying, retaining, and preserving, stabilizing, protecting and maintaining, repairing, and replacement
    b. Identifying, retaining, and preserving, protecting and maintaining, repairing, replacement, and stabilizing
    c. Identifying, retaining, and preserving, repairing, replacement, stabilizing, protecting and maintaining
    d. Identifying, repairing, replacement, stabilizing, protecting and maintaining, retaining, and preserving

56. After code research, an architect discovers an exposed wood stair in a historic building has to be fire rated. Which of the following procedure is recommended? **Check the two that apply.**
    a. Enclosing the wood stair with fire-resistant sheathing required by codes
    b. Upgrading historic stairway so that it is not damaged or obscured
    c. Adding a new stairway or elevator to meet health and safety codes in a manner that preserves adjacent character-defining features and spaces
    d. Installing sensitively designed fire suppression systems, such as sprinkler systems that result in retention of historic features and finishes

57. According to *The Secretary of the Interior's Standards for the Treatment of Historic Properties*, which of the following treatments are appropriate for a building individually listed in the National Register? **Check the two that apply.**
    a. Preservation
    b. Restoration
    c. Rehabilitation
    d. Reconstruction

58. A contractor submits structural steel shop drawings for the architect's review. The architect forwards the structural steel shop drawings to the structural engineer. Both the architect and the structural engineer have reviewed and marked up the shop drawings. The structural engineer also stamps and signs the shop drawings. After the structural steel members are installed in the field, per the approved shop drawings, the contractor notices the structural columns are too long, and will NOT achieve the roof slope required by the roof plans. The contractor submits a change order of $22,000 and one extra week of construction time for adjusted the structural columns. What is a proper action for the architect?
    a. Approves the change order and back charges the cost to the structural engineer.
    b. Approves the change order and submits a claim to her professional liabilities insurance company and to the structural engineer's professional liabilities insurance company.
    c. Negotiates with the contractor to reduce the amount of change order, obtains the owner's approval and then approves the change order.
    d. Denies the change order.

59. The principal AIA documents A201 family includes:
    a. Some documents in the A series, like agreement between owner and contractor
    b. Some documents in the A series, like agreement between owner and contractor and agreement between contractor and subcontractor
    c. Some documents in the A series, like agreement between owner and contractor and agreement between contractor and subcontractor, and some documents in the B series, like agreement between owner and architect
    d. Some documents in the A series, like agreement between owner and contractor and agreement between contractor and subcontractor, some documents in the B series, like agreement between owner and architect, and some documents in the C series, like agreement between architect and consultant

60. A security alarm consultant is installing wiring and equipment, and notices conflicts with HVAC ductwork and electrical conduits. What should the consultant do?
    a. Notify the architect only.
    b. Notify the mechanical engineer only.
    c. Notify the electrical engineer only.
    d. Notify the architect, the mechanical engineer, and the electrical engineer.

61. Per A201–2007, General Conditions of the Contract for Construction, which of the following tasks should the contractor complete? **Check the four that apply.**
    a. Prepare a punch list.
    b. Issue notice of substantial completion.
    c. Issue notice of final completion.
    d. Prepare the Certificate of Completion (C of O).
    e. Prepare the final change order.
    f. Prepare the final certificate of payment.
    g. Provide certificates of insurances and warranty.

62. At the end of the schematic design phase for a mixed-use building, the owner lost a major tenant and delayed the project. It took the owner six months to find another tenant and restart the project. Based on AIA document B101, which of the following should the architect have done during the six-month project suspension? **Check the three that apply.**
    a. Request payment for schematic design.
    b. Request an advance fee for design development and construction documents.
    c. Prepare a final bid package before ceasing work.
    d. Help the owner to find another tenant.
    e. Request payment for expenses incurred by the interruption of the architect's services.
    f. Submit a revised project schedule for when the project is resumed.

63. Which of the following are typically part of the submittal package to the planning department? **Check the six that apply.**
    a. architectural site plan
    b. building elevations
    c. landscape planting plans
    d. landscape irrigation plans
    e. survey plans
    f. site grading plans
    g. specifications
    h. site electrical plans

64. During the construction phase, the owner issues changes that will require six additional footings. The additional cost will be _____ based on the following information (Round to the nearest whole dollar.):
    - Size of each footing: 4' x 4' x 28'
    - Labor cost: $185 per cubic yard
    - Material cost including reinforcement: $235 per cubic yard
    - Miscellaneous equipment cost: $3 per cubic yard
    - Contractor's overhead and profit: 12%

65. An owner has purchased 70,000-square-feet of vacant land, and wants to develop it into a seven-home subdivision. Based on AIA document B101, what steps should the architect take when the owner provides an initial budget? **Check the three that apply.**
    a. Check the budget against the program.
    b. Check the budget against a construction budget handbook.
    c. Ask the owner to add some money for contingency.
    d. Start design plans based on the budget.
    e. Check the budget against the schedule.
    f. Check the budget against market conditions.

66. What should an architect do if there are conflicts in the state, county and, city codes?
    a. Follow the city code.
    b. Follow the adopted local code.
    c. Follow the ICC model code.
    d. Follow the most restrictive code.
    e. Follow the most restrictive adopted code.
    f. Ask ICC for clarification.

67. Several details are missing from the bid documents because of a concealed condition. The full scope of the work cannot be determined until demolition work is in progress. What strategies should the architect use to limit the cost increase during construction? **Check the two that apply.**
    a. addenda
    b. bid alternatives
    c. bulletins
    d. architect's supplemental instruction
    e. construction change directives
    f. change orders
    g. unit prices

68. What are the best ways for an architect to coordinate with consultants' plans? **Check the two that apply.**
    a. checking consultants' progress plans
    b. having regular meetings with the consultants and exchanging progress plans
    c. conference calls with consultants involving visual aids
    d. sending out memos to consultants describing the project requirements

69. All of the following will affect an architect's project schedule except:
    a. building code updates
    b. client decision making
    c. the architect's available staff
    d. the structural engineer's available staff
    e. the city's plan check

70. A structural engineer would typically decide the locations of columns at which stage of a project?
    a. pre-design
    b. schematic design
    c. design development
    d. construction documents

71. Which of the following is best for short design projects with few participants and little interactions between activities?
    a. milestone charts
    b. bar charts
    c. critical path method (CPM)
    d. full wall schedule

72. Persons may not reap the benefits nor suffer the burdens of a contract to which they were not a party. This legal term is called
    a. privity
    b. agency
    c. indemnification
    d. exclusion

73. An architect uses the C401-2007, Standard Form of Agreement Between Architect and Consultant, to retain the service of a structural consultant. During construction, the building inspector discovers that the number of hold-downs specified on the plans is not sufficient to meet code. Who is responsible for the extra cost to add additional hold-downs?
    a. architect
    b. building inspector
    c. consultant
    d. contractor
    e. owner

74. Who decides the type of footing and foundation system to use for a building?
    a. geotechnical engineer
    b. civil engineer
    c. structural engineer
    d. architect
    e. owner

75. A barber shop will lose about $500 per day if the owner cannot occupy the shop on time. What is the best way for the owner to encourage the contractor to finish the barber shop project on schedule?
    a. a bonus provision
    b. an incentive clause
    c. using liquidated damages
    d. a penalty provision

76. Per B101, Standard Form of Agreement Between Owner and Architect, all of the following are reimbursable expenses except: (**Check the two that apply.**)
    a. printing costs
    b. mileage
    c. overseas phone calls
    d. the cost for preparing the original request for proposal
    e. structural engineer's fees

77. If an owner terminates her contact with an architect for convenience in a project, but still needs to use the plans for remodeling the project later, which of the following is correct? **Check the two that apply.**
    a. The owner needs to pay the architect a licensing fee to use the plans.
    b. The owner can use the plans without paying extra fees.
    c. The architect is liable for the owner's uses of the plans for remodeling.
    d. The architect is not liable for the owner's uses of the plans for remodeling.

78. Which of the following is part of the A201 family of documents?
    a. A101, Standard Form of Agreement Between Owner and Contractor - Stipulated Sum
    b. A201, General Conditions of the Contract for Construction
    c. B101, Standard Form of Agreement Between Owner and Architect
    d. C401, Standard Form of Agreement Between Architect and Consultant
    e. all of the above
    f. none of the above

79. What does standard of care mean in B101, Standard Form of Agreement Between Owner and Architect? **Check the two that apply.**
    a. It means the architect needs to provide the highest standard of care and service to a client.
    b. It means the architect needs to provide an average standard of care and service to a client.
    c. It means the architect needs to provide the care that is ordinarily provided by architects practicing under the same or similar circumstances.
    d. It means the architect needs to provide the minimum standard of care and service to a client.

80. Per B101, Standard Form of Agreement Between Owner and Architect, the owner needs to provide all of the following except: **Check the two that apply.**
    a. a survey of the project site
    b. a program of the project
    c. certification from the owner's lender indicating that enough funds are available to pay for the design and construction of the project
    d. testing required by the contract documents
    e. a soils report
    f. local zoning ordinances

81. Per A101-2007, Standard Form of Agreement Between Owner and Contractor - Stipulated Sum, if the date of commencement for a project is March 1, and the project needs to be substantially completed in 90 days, when is the target substantial completion date?
    a. May 25
    b. May 29
    c. June 21
    d. June 25

82. An architect is designing a casino, and needs the assistance of a building codes consultant. When should the consultant be brought on board?
    a. pre-design stage
    b. schematic design stage
    c. design development stage
    d. construction document stage

83. Which of the following consultants are typically placed under the owner's contract? **Check the two that apply.**
    a. survey engineer
    b. civil engineer
    c. landscape architect
    d. structural engineer
    e. electrical engineer
    f. mechanical engineer
    g. plumbing engineer

B. Case Study

Questions 84 through 95 refer to the following case study. See figure 3.4 though figure 3.7 for information necessary to answer the questions.

1). Directions

An owner asks you to design a two-story custom home. Your floor plans should be responsive to given program and code requirements and should reflect principles of sound design logic. Adequate and code-compliant circulation should be provided, and the orientation of the building should be responsive to site influences.

2). Code & Site Information

Comply with the following code requirements. These are the ONLY code-related criteria you are required to use.

APN: 1234-567-890

Legal Description: PM 123-45-67 LOT 3

Zoning Designation: Residential

Front Yard Setback: 20', but needs to be 25' if the garage door is facing the front

Side Yard Setback: one is 5', the other is 12', but each side yard setback width shall be maintained for the whole length

Rear Yard Setback: 20', but the 2nd floor should be 25'

Height Limitation: 35'

Maximum Number of Stories: 2

Floor Area Ratio (FAR): none

Coverage Ratio: 40% of buildable areas, not the entire site. buildable areas are areas with 1 to 4 or less slope.

Lot Size: 14,457 s.f.

Easement Areas (including city horse trail): 4,731 s.f.

Existing Areas with more than 1 to 4 slope: 843 s.f.

First Floor Area: 2,096 s.f.

Garage Area: 629 s.f.

Second Floor Area: 1,898 s.f.

Total Area: 4,623 s.f. (including 629 s.f. of garage area)

3). Program
- Design a two-story single-family home with a square footage of approximately 3,500 s.f. to 4,000 s.f. on an approximately 14,400 s.f. lot. Develop details for the design work. Prepare city submittal plans.
- Review CC&R provided by the owner and prepare HOA submittal plans if necessary.

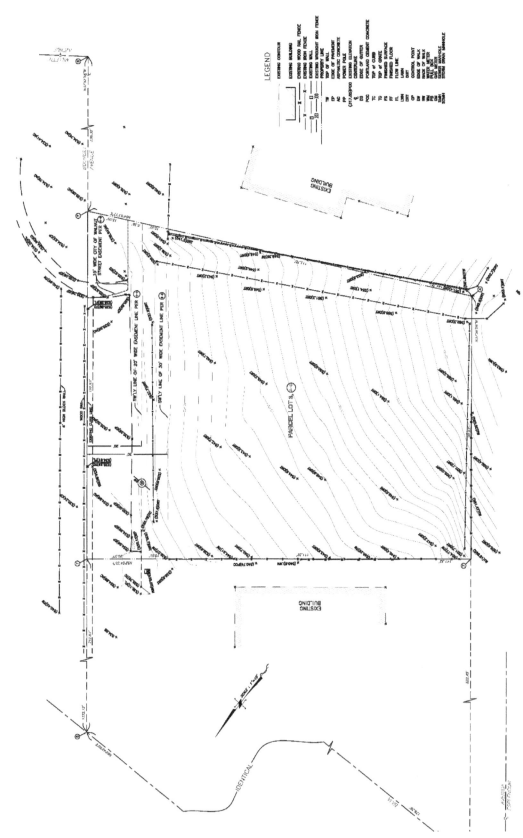

Figure 3.4   Site Topography Survey

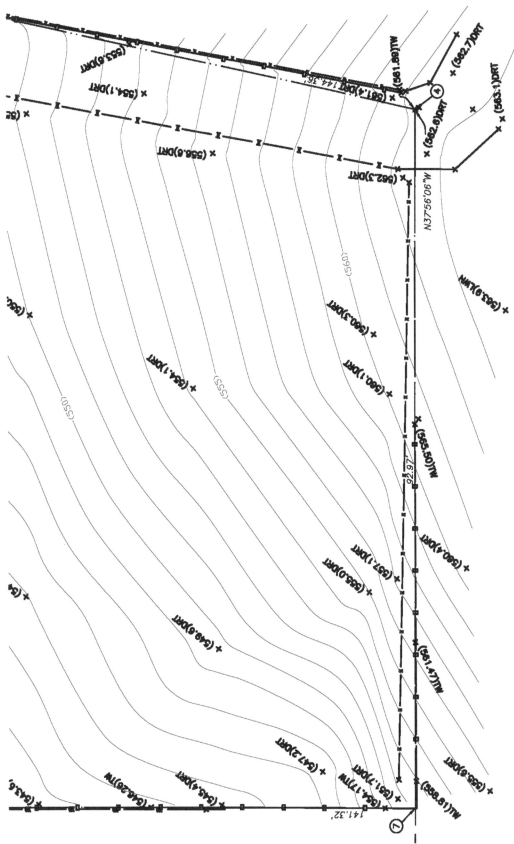

Figure 3.5 Enlarged Topo Survey

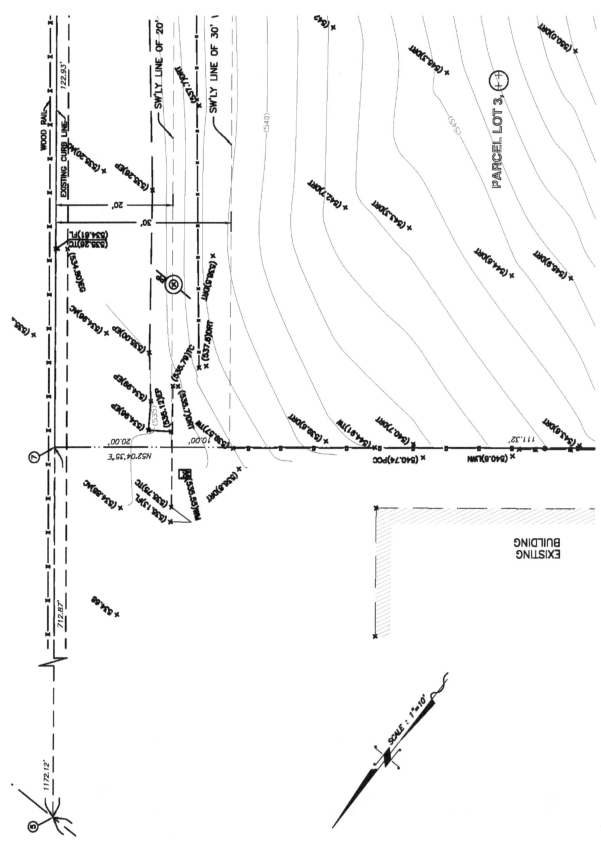

Figure 3.6 Enlarged Topo Survey

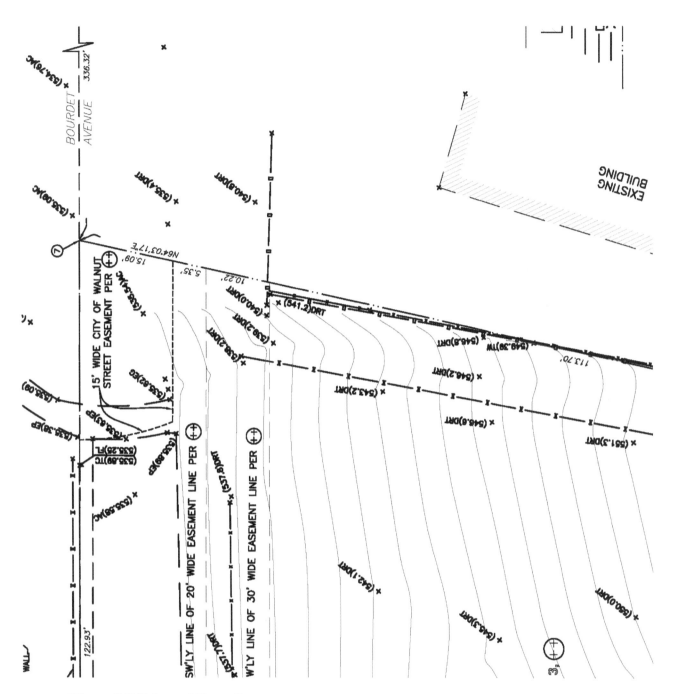

Figure 3.7 Enlarged Topo Survey

84. Per A201, General Conditions of the Contract for Construction, the surveyor is typically hired by the:
    a. owner
    b. architect
    c. contractor
    d. city

85. Based on the site survey plan, the site is:
    a. higher on the south, and slopes toward the north
    b. higher on the north, and slopes toward the south
    c. higher on the east, and slopes toward the west
    d. higher on the west, and slopes toward the east

86. During the excavation, the workers discovered an 18-inch-diameter storm drain. Further research revealed a 20-feet-wide storm drain easement. The easement is along the south boundary and was shown on the city storm drain plan, but the city did not record the easement with the county recorder's office. This discovery caused substantial design and construction delay and involved extra construction cost. Who is responsible for the extra construction cost? **Check the two that apply.**
    a. owner
    b. architect
    c. contractor
    d. city
    e. surveyor
    f. the party that hired the surveyor

87. Because the site is sloped and has an elevation change of close to 30', the architect suggested to design the building stepping down the slope in order to reduce the amount of cut and fill and the costs associated with this. The owner rejected the architect's suggestion and asked the architect to create a levelled area and to place the building there. What should the architect do? **Check the two that apply.**
    a. Refuse to follow the owner's instruction and cancel the contract because the owner's suggestion is against best management practice.
    b. Educate the owner and convince him to accept the architect's suggestion.
    c. Contact the city and ask the city building official to assist the architect to convince the owner to accept the architect's suggestion.
    d. Follow the owner's instruction and document the owner's rejection of the architect's suggestion.

88. What is the site coverage ratio?
    a. 26%
    b. 31%
    c. 37%
    d. 43%

89. Because of the missing easement on the survey plan, the owner has incurred extra costs. He is frustrated, and tells the architect that since he is running out of the money, he cannot pay the architectural fees now, but will pay the architect later when he gets extra funding. What should the architect do? **Check the two that apply.**
    a. Be cool and just wait until the owner has money to get paid.
    b. Give the owner a seven-day written notice of stopping the project.
    c. Give the owner written notice and then suspend services.
    d. Give the owner written notice and then terminate services.
    e. Set up a meeting with the owner to find a common ground and arrange for a payment plan.

90. Which section of the geotechnical report will give the structural engineer information on footing and foundation design?
    a. site location and project development
    b. field investigation
    c. soils condition
    d. conclusions and recommendations

91. At the construction document stage, which of the following typically requires a submittal to a separate department?
    a. civil plans
    b. architectural plans
    c. structural plans
    d. electrical, mechanical, and plumbing plans
    e. energy calculations

92. Which of the following should be included in the architect's feasibility studies? **Check the two that apply.**
    a. local zoning ordinances
    b. proposed design schedule
    c. recommendation for financing the project
    d. recommendation for selecting the geotechnical and civil engineers

93. What is the least important question the architect should ask.
    a. Do the local codes permit such use?
    b. What are the setback requirements for front yard, side yards, and rear yard?
    c. Does the building need to be sprinklered?
    d. What is the site coverage ratio?
    e. What are the parking requirements?
    f. What is the maximum building height?

94. If the owner wants to expedite the project, which delivery methods should he choose? **Check the two that apply.**
    a. bidding
    b. design-build
    c. construction manager as adviser
    d. bridging

95. Two architectural firms are involved with a project. ArchiteG, Inc is the owner's consultant, and Smith and Associates is hired as a design-build firm to perform the design and a portion of the construction services. Project tasks include:
    * design charrettes
    * outline specifications
    * selection of the mechanical systems
    * coordination of geotechnical studies
    * RFP responses
    * reviews and comments on progress plans
    * evaluation of payment application
    * preparation of plans for permit
    * review of shop drawings
    * development of overall project budget
    * organization of pre-proposal conference for subcontractors

    In the following table, place the aforementioned tasks in the correct columns and applicable project phase.

Project Phase	ArchiteG, Inc.	Smith and Associates
Pre-design		
Design		
Construction		

Chapter Four

ARE Mock Exam Solutions for
Project Management (PjM) Division

A. Mock Exam Answers and Explanations: Multiple-Choice (MC)

Note: If you answer 60% of the questions correctly, you pass the MC Section of the exam.

1. Answer: a
   A multiple prime is the correct answer. A **multiple prime** is the arrangement in which the owner contracts directly with several contractors instead of a single prime contractor.

   The following are the incorrect answers and their definitions:
   - **an associated firm:** a firm controlled by another firm to an extent that is less than a subsidiary
   - **a joint venture**: for a finite time, two firms join together to develop a new entity and new assets by contributing equity
   - **partnering**: to associate as partners

2. Answer: c
   Completing a feasibility study is the best choice.

   The other choices listed are good suggestions, but they are NOT the best.
   - compare the cost of the two choices
   - seek LEED certification for the home
   - complete a life safety study

3. Answer: b
   Blocking and stacking are terms used in programming. **Stacking** is an activity of programming, in which floors or areas of floors are assigned to departments based upon their adjacency and support requirements.

   Blocking is an activity of programming, in which <u>departments are assigned</u> to a particular area of a floor based upon adjacency and support requirements.

   The following are incorrect answers:
   - terms used in masonry construction
   - terms used in structural calculations
   - terms used in design development

4. Answer: b
The first C in CC&R stands for Covenants. **CC&R is Covenants, Conditions and Restrictions**. They are limitations and rules set by developer, a builder, neighborhood association, and/or homeowner association. All townhomes, condos, as well as most planned unit developments, and established neighborhoods have CC&Rs.

5. Answer: a, b and d
The following can cause mold inside a building wall:
- poor ventilation
- poor drainage
- organic feedstock

The following are incorrect answers:
- flashing (Lack of proper flashing can cause mold.)
- EIFS (Lack of proper flashing and drainage can cause mold in a wall with an EIFS system, although not in EIFS itself.)

6. Answer: a, b, e, and f
An architectural project program should include the following:
- a basis of design (BOD)
- owner project requirements (OPR)
- a budget
- type and quantity of spaces

The followings are incorrect answers:
- type of structural system (This should be part of design development decisions.)
- type of HVAC system (This should be part of design development decisions.)

7. Answer: b
The project schedule in figure 3.1 is known as a critical path method (CPM).

A Gantt chart is a type of bar chart used frequently in project schedules. **Program evaluation and review technique (PERT)** is a statistical tool, used in project management. **Project cycle method (PCM)** or **Project cycle management method (PCM)** is a tool to manage the whole project cycle.

8. Answer: d
The total numbers of days needed to finish the project per the project schedule in figure 3.1 is 38. The total number of days is determined by the critical path, which is shown as bolded arrows in figure 3.1. Each solid arrow represents an activity. The numbered circles are beginning and/or end point of an activity. *All activities leading to a circle must be finished before you can go to the next step.* You need to pick the *worst* case leading to each circle to calculate the time needed to finish an activity.

9. Answer: c
    The dashed arrows in figure 3.1 are known as dummies. **Dummies** indicate relationship. They are not activities and have no duration.

    The following are incorrect answers or **distracters**:
    *   knots
    *   paths
    *   processes

10. Answer: b
    After the award of a construction contract, the contractor shall submit a schedule of construction for architect review.

    The following are incorrect answers or **distracters**:
    *   a punch list (The contractor shall submit this at the end of construction.)
    *   a list of potential change order (The contractor does NOT have to submit this.)
    *   a change order log (The contractor does NOT have to submit this.)
    *   a submittal log (The contractor does NOT have to submit this.)

11. Answer: a
    Unit price is the most accurate type of estimate.

    The following are incorrect answers or **distracters**:
    *   An estimate based on the construction cost of similar buildings
    *   cost of building systems
    *   historical data of the same type of construction

12. Answer: b and c
    The best solutions for the architect to get the job while still protecting the interests of her firm are:
    *   Transfer ownership of the architectural plans and specifications to the owner and require the owner to sign a waiver releasing the architect of the liabilities for unauthorized use of the documents.
    *   Negotiate with the owner and try to seek joint-ownership of the plans and specifications.

    Since the owner wants the architect to transfer ownership of the architectural plans and specifications to the owner as a prerequisite to granting the design contract, the architect is unlikely to get the job if she chooses the following two options:
    *   Tell the owner that the architect should have copyrights of all documents generated by the architect per the AIA documents.
    *   Refuse the owner's request.

13. Answer: b and c

The following are characteristic of fast-track projects:

- The design phase overlaps the construction phase; construction often starts before the plans are complete.
- Multiple bid packages are involved, such as the foundation bid package, the superstructure bid package, and the exterior enclosure bid package.

The following are incorrect answers or **distracters**:

- The design phase occurs before the construction phase.
- One bid package is utilized to simplify the construction process.

14. Answer: a and d

The following are the most important considerations in an architect/owner contract:

- scope of services
- architectural service fees

The following may NOT even be discussed in an architect/owner contract: (They are the incorrect answers.)

- consultants
- type of construction

15. Answer: d

A health department plan check fee is typically not required for a new library building because a library does NOT sell food. Health department plan check fees are required for buildings that have food processing departments or sell foods, including pre-packaged food such as candy.

The following fees are typically required for a new library building plan check as well as on most other new buildings:

- a planning department plan check fee
- a building department plan check fee
- a fire department plan check fee
- a school district fee
- a drainage fee

16. Answer: a

The cost for a geotechnical survey is typically borne by the owner.

The following are incorrect answers:

- architect
- contractor
- federal government

17. Answer: e

The best way to reduce the number of change orders is to finish coordination and quality control before issuing the bid package.

Issuing multiple bid packages will NOT reduce the number of change orders.

The following will reduce the number of change orders, but they are NOT the best way, and therefore the incorrect answers:
- hold regular coordination meetings
- use an outside peer review service
- have owners review the plans

18. Answer: a and b

Hiring qualified employees and communication among employees are effective ways to improve the quality of construction documents.

The following are helpful, but they are NOT the best way, and therefore the incorrect answers:
- have owners review the plans
- use outside consultants

19. Answer: b

The AIA Document C401-2007 includes a new flow-down provision that extends the responsibilities and rights contracted between the architect and owner, down to the agreement made between the consultants and the architect.

The following are incorrect answers:
- the owner and the contractor
- the architect and the contractor
- none of the above

20. Answer: a

Outline specifications during the schematic design stage are typically broken down into divisions.

The following are incorrect answers:
- disciplines
- costs
- the critical path method

21. Answer: b
Bid alternates to choose between stone veneer and brick veneer, double-glazing and single-glazing, and clay roof tiles and asphalt shingles are most likely the architect's attempt to control construction costs.

The following are incorrect answers:
- incorporate environmental friendly options
- anticipate HOA CC&R requirements (HOA stands for Home Owner's Association; CC&R stands for Covenants, Conditions and Restrictions.)
- address neighborhood concerns

22. Answer: a
A Specific Plan is typically developed or paid for by the city.

The City of San Marcos, California has a very good definition of a General Plan and a Specific Plan. This definition also applies to other cities.
"The **General Plan** is the long-term policy guide for the physical, economic, and environmental growth of a city and represents the community's vision of its ultimate physical growth."

"A **Specific Plan** is a comprehensive planning document that guides the development of a defined geographic area in a mix of uses including residential, commercial, industrial, schools, parks, and open space."

See the following link:
http://www.ci.san-marcos.ca.us/index.aspx?page=323

The following are incorrect answers:
- civil engineer
- architect
- structural engineer
- owner
- contractor

23. Answer: e
EIR stands for Environmental Impact Report. The owner typically pays for an EIR.

The following are incorrect answers:
- city
- civil engineer
- architect
- structural engineer
- contractor

24. Answer: c

During the construction documents phase of work, the architect receives the plan check corrections. The following is the most effective way to coordinate the engineering consultant's work:

- Review and mark up the plan check corrections, mark up the consultants' plans per the list, and then send only the relevant part of the plan check corrections list and the marked-up sheets of the consultants' plans to the related consultants.

The following are incorrect answers:

- Send the entire plan check corrections list to all the consultants, and then start to review the plan check corrections list. *Note: This is NOT efficient because you are asking the consultants to deal with the same thing twice.*
- Review the plan check corrections list first, and then send only the relevant part of the plan check corrections list to the related consultants. *Note: This is NOT efficient because you will have to send the marked-up sheets of the consultants' plans to the related consultants later.*
- Review and mark up the plan check corrections, mark up the consultants' plans per the list, and then send only the relevant part of the plan check corrections list and entire set of the consultants' plans with the mark-ups to the related consultants. *Note: This is NOT efficient because the consultants should already have a complete set of plans for coordination, and you do NOT need to re-send the entire set of the consultants' plans with the mark-ups.*

25. Answer: b and c

The following items are true according to A101–2007, Standard Form of Agreement Between Owner and Contractor where the basis of payment is a Stipulated Sum:

- Arbitration is binding in most states.
- Mediation is mandatory.

Mediation is NOT binding.

Arbitration is NOT handled by AIA, but instead by the American Arbitration Association (AAA).

26. Answer: a and b

Governing agencies regulate the development of projects through:

- General plans
- Specific plans

See answer 44 on pages 75 and 76 for definitions of these terms as well as a website link for further information.

The following are incorrect answers:

- CC&R (This is used by Home Owners' Associations, or HOA.)
- plumbing permits (These are used to regulate specific buildings, and are NOT used for the development of projects.)

27. Answer: a, b and c
    The following will affect a project's schedule:
    - the client (The client's ability to make decision in a timely manner has a significant impact on the schedule.)
    - the number of project team members (More people in the team can speed up the project.)
    - the architect (The experience of the architect or her associates will affect a project's schedule.)

    Insurance is less likely to affect a project's schedule.

28. Answer: a, b and d
    The following will restrict a project's development:
    - the municipal codes
    - the building codes
    - the fire department

    The experience of construction workers is less likely to restrict a project's development.

29. Answer: b and d
    A soils report typically includes the following:
    - seismic considerations
    - footing and foundation design guidelines

    A soils report typically does not include the following:
    - landscaping
    - utilities

    Please note the difference between a soils report and a site survey. A **soils report** is typically prepared by a soils engineer. Its main purpose is to explore the underground soil conditions and provide design recommendations and guidelines for the structural engineer.

    A **site survey** is typically prepared by a land surveyor or a civil engineer. Its main purpose is to document the existing surface conditions at the site, including contours, landscaping, easements, existing buildings and utilities, etc.

30. Answer: c
    The following is the correct order for arranging the units used in the Public Land Survey System (PLSS) in the US, from large to small:
    - check, township, section

    A **check** is a square parcel of land 576 square miles in area with 24-mile-long sides.
    A **township** is a square parcel of land 36 square miles in area with 6-mile-long sides.
    A **section** is a square parcel of land 1 square mile in area with 1-mile-long sides.

31. Answer: a and b
    The following are measures to improve water quality:
    - **retention pond** or **retention basin** (This is also called a **wet pond**, **wet detention basin**, or **lake fail**, and is used to hold water permanently.) See the following link: http://en.wikipedia.org/wiki/Retention_basin
    - **detention pond** or **detention basin** (This is also called a **dry pond**, **holding pond**, or, **dry detention basin** if no permanent pool of water exists. It is used to hold water for a limited time.) See the following link: http://en.wikipedia.org/wiki/Detention_basin

    The following are incorrect answers:
    - concrete swale
    - trench drain

32. Answer: b
    The following is the best method to reduce asbestos exposure in an existing building:
    - Keep asbestos-containing materials in place without disturbing it.

    The following are incorrect answers:
    - Remove the asbestos. (This can disturb the asbestos-containing materials and make matter worse.)
    - Seal off the spaces with asbestos containing materials. (This is not practical.)
    - Ban children from rooms with asbestos containing materials. (This is not practical.)

33. Answer: d
    Pay attention to the word "not."
    ADA does <u>not</u> regulate a building's height, and is therefore the correct answer.

    The following are incorrect answers:
    - zoning codes
    - building codes
    - CC&R (Covenants, Conditions and Restrictions)

34. Answer: d
    Pay attention to the word "not."

    The following do <u>not</u> need to comply with ADA Accessibility Guidelines (ADAAG), and are therefore the correct answers:
    - a single-family home on a private property
    - a construction trailer

    A city hall building needs to comply with ADA Accessibility Guidelines (ADAAG).

35. Answer: a and c
    In a construction project, a contractor's insurance will pay for claims from the owner, if the owner waives his rights to sue for and recover from the contractor. This arrangement is an example of a **waiver of subrogation**, or an **exculpatory clause**.

    The following are incorrect answers:
    • an exclusive right
    • a waiver of abrogation (This is a distracter, and an invented term.)

36. Answer: a and d
    Per AIA Document B101-2007, the following regarding mediation is true:
    • Mediation shall always precede litigation. (See AIA Document B101-2007, 8.2.1, 8.2.4)
    • The parties shall share the mediation fees equally. (See AIA Document B101-2007, 8.2.3)

    The following are incorrect answers:
    • The prevailing party will be reimbursed for the mediation fees.
    • Arbitration shall always precede mediation.

37. Answer: a and c
    Eminent domain means the state has the power to seize a citizen's private property, without the owner's consent and use the property for the public benefits. The state has to pay a fair market value to the owner for the loss of the property.

    See the following link:
    http://en.wikipedia.org/wiki/Eminent_domain

    The following can use eminent domain to acquire land for project development:
    • a public school
    • an interstate freeway

    The following are incorrect answers:
    • a toll road (These are typically owned by a private owner instead of a public entity.)
    • a shopping center

38. Answer: b
    Rehabilitation receives the most tax incentive with regard to historical buildings.

    See the following related link:
    http://www.nps.gov/tps/tax-incentives/taxdocs/about-tax-incentives.pdf
    http://www.nps.gov/history/hps/tps/tax/rehabstandards.htm

- **Preservation** is the process of preserving monuments, buildings, etc.
- **Rehabilitation** is defined as "the process of returning a property to a state of utility, through repair or alteration, which makes possible an efficient contemporary use while preserving those portions and features of the property which are significant to its historic, architectural, and cultural values." The Standards for Rehabilitation (codified in 36 CFR 67 for use in the Federal Historic Preservation Tax Incentives program) address this most prevalent treatment.
- **Restoration** is work performed on a building to return it to a previous state.
- **Reconstruction** is the process of rebuilding a historic building that has been destroyed, based on historic records, etc.

39. Answer: a

The following is the correct order to arrange building types based on their building efficiencies, from high to low:

- department store, office, apartment, hospital

Building efficiency is the ratio of area that is assigned to a function (NASF) to gross square feet (GSF).

Building efficiency = NASF/GSF

A building with less supportive spaces is more efficient, and has a high building efficiency.

40. Answer: a

Buildings codes, ADA, municipal codes, and EPA Codes of Federal Regulations are laws, because they have gone through the legislation process, but reference guides by USGBC are NOT laws. They are rules set by the USGBC. The USGBC has NO legal authority like the other governing agencies.

LEED standards are voluntary. You choose to obey the rules when you seek certification for a building, but these rules are NOT laws.

Note:
NCARB has started to draw 23% to 29% or 19 to 25 of the questions of the PPP ARE exam from Environmental, Social & Economic Issues. We include some questions on green buildings and LEED to help you to meet this new challenge.

If you are weak on this subject, you are more than welcome to check out our LEED Exam Guide series and other books. They are available as printed books and PDF eBooks at our website:
http://www.GreenExamEducation.com

You can preview up to 20% of all our books' content at:
http://books.google.com/

Please also see our website for more FREE tips and downloads:
http://www.GreenExamEducation.com

41. Answer: c, d, and e
Increasing the site coverage will increase impervious area and will increase stormwater runoff. Increasing the FAR may or may NOT increase impervious area. Porous pavement will help recharge the groundwater thereby reducing stormwater runoff, and high-albedo (high-reflectivity) materials will increase reflectivity to alleviate the urban "heat island" effect. Vegetated roofs and retention ponds can also reduce stormwater runoff and alleviate the urban "heat island" effect.

42. Answer: b
Recycled materials can protect virgin materials, but may require more energy to process, can increase traffic, and increase MEP cost.

43. Answer: f
Graywater is the household water that has not come into contact with the kitchen sink or toilet waste.

See USGBC Definitions at the link below:

https://www.usgbc.org/ShowFile.aspx?DocumentID=5744

44. Answer: a and d
Read the question carefully; it is asking for the WRONG statements.

45. Answer: e
Life cycle cost analysis is unique to a LEED certified building. Hard costs, soft costs, and storm control costs are required by both a LEED certified building and a conventional building. "Life cycle analysis costs" is different from life cycle cost analysis, and is a distracter.

Life cycle cost analysis is an evaluation of a building's economic performance including operational and maintenance costs over the life of the product.

Life cycle analysis is the same as eco-balance, cradle-to-cradle analysis, or life cycle assessment. It is used to evaluate the environmental impact of a service or product.

46. Answer: d
Minimum energy performance is a prerequisite, not a credit. Emission measurement and radon alleviation are distracters.

47. Answer: c
Concerning ozone depletion potential (ODP): CFCs>HCFCs>HFCs. Therefore, HFCs have the lowest ODP.

48. Answer: a
Construction debris sent to a recycle facility is the only item that has been used by a consumer, and is therefore a post-consumer item.

49. Answer: b

   ISO 14000 evaluates the environmental performance of services and products. It includes Design for Environment, Life Cycle Assessment, and Environmental Labels and Declaration.

50. Answer:

   The following are steps to solve the problem concerning the labor schedule:

   1) **Remove design consultants' fee:**

      Architectural design fee = $210,000 – (35% x $210,000) = $136,500

   2) **Divided by the 3.0 company multiplier:**

      $$\frac{\$136,500}{3} = \$45,500$$

   3) **Calculate the weekly budget:**

      $$\frac{\$45,500}{8} = \$5,687.5$$

   4) **Allocate the principal's weekly hours to the labor schedule:**

      20% x 40 hours = 8 hours

      8 x $105 = $840 per week

   5) **Utilization of the Project Architect, Job Captain, and Drafter should be maximized:**

      ($40 + $30 + $20) x 40 =$3,600 per week

   6) **Calculate Project Manager's hours:**

      $5,687.5 - $840 - $3,600 = $1,247.5

      $$\frac{\$1,247.5}{50} = 24.95 \; hours$$

8	Available staff	Direct Rate	Weekly person-hour
20.95	Principal	$105	8
22.95	Project Manager	$50	24.95
24.95	Project Architect	$40	40
30	Job Captain	$30	40
40	Drafter	$20	40

Figure 4.1   Completed Labor Schedule

51. Answer: a, c, and e
    The following statements regarding the design-build approach are true:
    - It has been used for more than 4,000 years. (According to *the Architect's Handbook of Professional Practice*, or AHPP, the roots of design-build go back to Imhotep, the Egyptian architect and master builder who designed the Step Pyramid.
    - If an architect is leading a design-build project, she needs to be responsible for the accuracy of her consultant's work.
    - If an architect is leading a design-build project, she needs to schedule and control means and methods of construction.

52. Answer: d
    The owner eventually hires two architects.

    According to AHPP, bridged design-build is a special kind of project. In a bridged design-build project, the owner eventually hires two architects, one of which is part of a design-build team. The first architect develops preliminary design, a performance specification, and detailed criteria, and then passes the concept and criteria package to the design-build team.

    A contractor is *not* acting as a bridge between the architect and the owner.
    An architect is acting as a bridge between the owner and the design-build team, she is *not* acting as a bridge between the contractor and the owner.

53. Answer:
    See Figure 4.2. The extra weeks are shown as black in the column grid. Please note that the delay for bidding and permitting are concurrent, so they push back the start of construction by only four weeks. Two weeks must be added to the construction schedule. The new completion date will be six weeks later.

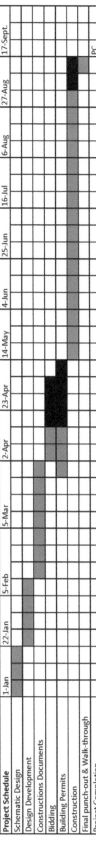

Figure 4.2   Revised Project Schedule

54. Answer: c

A new mechanical system is required to make a historic building functional. The following is recommended:

- Place the mechanical unit on the ground and enclose it with hedges.

The following are NOT recommended:

- Place the mechanical unit in the attic and remove a substantial amount of building materials.
- Place the mechanical unit in an existing masonry unit enclosure and cut through the existing masonry walls.
- Place the mechanical unit on the roof top and add additional beams and columns to support the unit

See page 50 of the PDF file for *The Secretary of the Interior's Standards for the Treatment of Historic Properties with Guidelines for Preserving, Rehabilitating Restoring & Reconstructing Historic Buildings* at the following links:
http://www.ironwarrior.org/ARE/Historic_Preservation/

55. Answer: a

The following procedure is recommended for historic building:

- Identifying, retaining, and preserving, stabilizing, protecting and maintaining, repairing, and replacement

See the PDF file for *The Secretary of the Interior's Standards for the Treatment of Historic Properties with Guidelines for Preserving, Rehabilitating Restoring & Reconstructing Historic Buildings* at the following links:
http://www.ironwarrior.org/ARE/Historic_Preservation/

56. Answer: b and c

After code research, an architect discovers an exposed wood stair in a historic building has to be fire rated. The following procedure are recommended:

- Upgrading historic stairway so that it is not damaged or obscured
- Adding a new stairway or elevator to meet health and safety codes in a manner that preserves adjacent character-defining features and spaces

The following procedures are NOT recommended:

- Enclosing the wood stair with fire-resistant sheathing required by codes (Covering character-defining wood features with fire-resistant sheathing which results in altering their visual appearance is NOT recommended.)
- Installing sensitively designed fire suppression systems, such as sprinkler systems that result in retention of historic features and finishes (This will NOT meet the exiting codes requirements.)

See page 59 of the PDF file for *The Secretary of the Interior's Standards for the Treatment of Historic Properties with Guidelines for Preserving, Rehabilitating Restoring & Reconstructing Historic Buildings* at the following links:
http://www.ironwarrior.org/ARE/Historic_Preservation/

57. Answer: a and b
According to *The Secretary of the Interior's Standards for the Treatment of Historic Properties*, the following treatments are appropriate for a building individually listed in the National Register:
*   Preservation
*   Restoration

The following treatments are inappropriate for a building individually listed in the National Register:
*   Rehabilitation (It is for buildings that contribute to the significance of a historic district but are NOT individually listed in the National Register)
*   Reconstruction (It is for re-creating a vanished or non-surviving building with new materials, primarily for interpretive purposes.)

See pages 1 and 2 of the PDF file for *The Secretary of the Interior's Standards for the Treatment of Historic Properties with Guidelines for Preserving, Rehabilitating Restoring & Reconstructing Historic Buildings* at the following links:
http://www.ironwarrior.org/ARE/Historic_Preservation/

58. Answer: d
The following is a proper action for the architect:
*   Denies the change order.

The following are improper action for the architect:
*   Approves the change order and back charges the cost to the structural engineer.
*   Approves the change order and submits a claim to her professional liabilities insurance company and to the structural engineer's professional liabilities insurance company.
*   Negotiates with the contractor to reduce the amount of change order, obtains the owner's approval and then approves the change order.

Per Article 4.2.7 of A201–2007, General Conditions of the Contract for Construction, an architect reviews submittals including shop drawings for conformance with information given and the design concept expressed in the construction documents. The review is NOT for the purpose of determining the accuracy and completeness of other details such as dimensions and quantities.

You can find AIA document A201–2007, General Conditions of the Contract for Construction, at the following link:
https://www.aiacontracts.org/

59. Answer: d

The principal AIA documents A201 family includes:

- Some documents in the A series, like agreement between owner and contractor and agreement between contractor and subcontractor, some documents in the B series, like agreement between owner and architect, and some documents in the C series, like agreement between architect and consultant

See Introduction of A201–2007, General Conditions of the Contract for Construction.

You can find AIA document A201–2007, General Conditions of the Contract for Construction, at the following link:
https://www.aiacontracts.org/

60. Answer: a

Notify the architect only.
According to C401-2007, Standard Form of Agreement Between Architect and Consultant, if a consultant notices any conflicts, she should promptly inform the architect. Notifying the mechanical engineer and/or the electrical engineer directly is not proper protocol, and will only create confusion.

61. Answer: a, b, c, and g

Per A201–2007, General Conditions of the Contract for Construction, the contractor is responsible for the following activities:

- Prepare a punch list.
- Issue notice of substantial completion.
- Issue notice of final completion.
- Provide certificates of insurances and warranty.

The contractor is *not* responsible for the following activities:

- Prepare the Certificate of Completion (C of O). This is prepared by the building department.
- Prepare the final change order. This is prepared by the architect.
- Prepare the final certificate of payment. This is prepared by the architect.

62. Answer: a, e, and f

Based on AIA document B101, the architect should have done the following during the six-month project suspension:

- Request payment for schematic design.
- Request payment for expenses incurred by the interruption of the architect's services.
- Submit a revised project schedule for when the project is resumed.

The following are incorrect answers:
- Request an advance fee for design development and construction documents. (This is not wise. The architect should suspend the service instead.)
- Prepare a final bid package before ceasing work. (The architect should suspend the service instead.)
- Help the owner to find another tenant (This is outside the scope of the architect's work.)

63. Answer: a, b, c, e, f, and h
    The following are typically part of the submittal package to the planning department:
    - architectural site plan
    - building elevations
    - landscape planting plans
    - survey plans
    - site grading plans
    - site electrical plans

    The following are typically *not* part of the submittal package to the planning department:
    - landscape irrigation plans (These are typically part of the construction documents submitted to the building department.)
    - specifications (These are typically part of the bid documents issued to the bidders.)

64. Answer: During the construction phase, the owner issues changes that will requires six additional footings. The additional cost will be _____ $47,168 _____ based on the information provided in the question. This figure is round to the nearest whole dollar and is solved by the steps below.

    1) Determine the total volume of the additional footing:
       (4' x 4' x 28') x 6 locations = 2,688 cubic feet = 99.56 cubic yard
       Note: 1 cubic yard = 27 cubic feet

    2) Determine the total cost of the footing, including labor, materials, and miscellaneous equipment cost:
       ($185 + $235 + $3) x 99.56 cubic yard = $42,113.88

    3) Add the contractor's overhead and profit:
       $42,113.88 x 112% = $47,167.55

    4) Round to the nearest whole dollar:
       $47,168

65. Answer: a, e, and f
Based on AIA document B101, the architect should check the budget against the program, schedule, and market conditions.

The following are incorrect answers:
- Check the budget against a construction budget handbook. (A construction budget handbook is not very accurate and may not reflect the local conditions.)
- Ask the owner to add some money for contingency. (The architect needs to check the budget against the program, schedule, and market conditions first to see if the budget is adequate.)
- Start design plans based on the budget. (The architect needs to understand the budget and its impact before developing any plans.)

66. Answer: e
When there are code conflicts, an architect always needs to follow the most restrictive adopted code.

67. Answer: b and g
The architect should use bid alternatives and unit prices to limit the cost increase during construction.
- **Bid alternatives** list alternate options which add or deduct items of work.
- **Unit prices** are prices for each unit, including materials and labor.

The following do not limit the cost increase during construction or are limited in doing so:
- **Addenda** are used to issue changes during bidding.
- **Bulletins** are used to issue changes during construction.
- **Architect's supplemental instruction** is an invented term used as a distractor. **Supplemental instructions** are modifications to the general condition of a contract and have limited impact on cost.
- **Construction change directives** are used to issue changes during construction when the owner and contractor cannot agree on the price of the changes, and the work must proceed.
- **Change Orders** are used to use to adjust the project cost because of changes during construction.

68. Answer: b and c
The best ways for an architect to coordinate with consultants' plans are:
- having regular meetings with the consultants and exchanging progress plans, and
- conference calls with consultants involving visual aids.

Both of the aforementioned tactics involve two-way communications and visual aids or plans, which are the best ways to coordinate.

The following are one-way communications, and are less effective:
- checking consultants' progress plans, and
- sending out memos to consultants describing the project requirements.

69. Answer: d
    The following will not affect an architect's project schedule:
    • the structural engineer's available staff
    The structural engineer's available staff will affect the structural engineer's project schedule, not the architect's.

    All of the following will affect an architect's project schedule:
    • building code updates (The architect will need more time to study and incorporate the code updates.)
    • client decision making (This can hold up the architect's project if the client cannot make decisions in a timely manner.)
    • the architect's available staff
    • the city's plan check (The speed at which this is processed, has a direct impact on an architect's project schedule.)

70. Answer: c
    A structural engineer would typically decide the locations of columns during the design development stage of a project.

    The schematic design needs to be finalized and approved by the client before a structural engineer can determine the locations of columns.

    At the construction document stage, a structural engineer would calculate and determine the exact size of columns and beams.

71. Answer: a
    Per *the Architect's Handbook of Professional Practice*, or AHPP, **milestone charts** are best for short design projects with few participants and little interactions between activities. This type of chart only shows completion dates.
    • **Bar charts**, also known as **Gantt charts** or **harmonograms**, are the most widely used tool among architects. These charts have a list of tasks along the left side of the page. Horizontal bars indicate the start and finish dates of each task.
    • **Critical path method (CPM)** is often used by contractors to schedule construction sequences. It shows the interrelationships among project tasks.
    • **A full wall schedule** encourages all team members participate in developing the project schedule, and facilitates the discussions of responsibilities, deadlines, and tasks.

72. Answer: a

Persons may not reap the benefits nor suffer the burdens of a contract to which they were not a party. The legal term is **privity**. For example, if a consumer bought a light bulb from a retailer who had originally bought them from the manufacturer, then, if the light bulb is faulty, the consumer should sue the retailer, not the manufacturer.

- **Agency** is an organization that provides a service that involves facilitating transactions between two other parties.
- **Indemnification** is to guard or secure against anticipated loss.
- **Exclusion** is the process or state of being excluded, or an item or risk not covered by a contract or insurance policy.

73. Answer: c

The consultant is responsible for the extra cost to add additional hold-downs. Per C401-2007, Standard Form of Agreement Between Architect and Consultant, the consultant is responsible for code compliance in their portion of the work.

74. Answer: c

A geotechnical engineer can suggest the type of the footing and foundation system to use for a building, but the structural engineer makes the final decision.

75. Answer: c

Using **liquidated damages** is the best way for the owner to encourage the contractor to finish the barber shop project on schedule. Liquidated damages are damages agreed upon in advance by both parties, and do *not* need to be accompanied by a bonus provision.

- An **incentive clause** can be either positive or negative; it typically includes the description and amount of the incentive.
- A **penalty provision** *must* be accompanied by a **bonus provision**, otherwise, it is unenforceable, even this does not guarantee it will be enforceable.

76. Answer: d and e

Pay attention to the word "except."

Per B101, Standard Form of Agreement Between Owner and Architect, the following are *not* reimbursable expenses and therefore the correct answers:

- the cost for preparing the original request for proposal (This is part of the office overhead, not a reimbursable expense)
- structural engineer's fees (This should be part of the professional design fee, not a reimbursable expense.)

Per B101, Standard Form of Agreement Between Owner and Architect, all of the following are reimbursable expenses:

- printing costs
- mileage
- overseas phone calls

77. Answer: a and d

If an owner terminates her contact with an architect for convenience in a project, but still needs to use the plans for remodeling the project later, the following is correct:

- The owner needs to pay the architect a licensing fee to use the plans if she terminates her contact with an architect for convenience in a project, OR if the architect terminates because of the owner's suspension of the project.

- The architect is not liable for the owner's uses of the plans for remodeling. Use of the architect's instrument of service (the plans) where the architect is not involved, following the owner's termination for convenience, OR if the architect terminates because of the owner's suspension of the project, will be without liability to the architect.

See B101, Standard Form of Agreement Between Owner and Architect, for more information.

78. Answer: e

All of the following are part of the A201 family of documents:

- A101, Standard Form of Agreement Between Owner and Contractor - Stipulated Sum
- A201, General Conditions of the Contract for Construction
- B101, Standard Form of Agreement Between Owner and Architect
- C401, Standard Form of Agreement Between Architect and Consultant

These documents, as well as, **A102**, Standard Form of Agreement Between Owner and Contractor (Cost plus fee, with GMP), **A103**, Standard Form of Agreement Between Owner and Contractor (Cost plus fee, without GMP), **A401**, Standard Form of Agreement Between Contractor and Subcontractor, **B103**, Standard Form of Agreement Between Owner and Architect for a Large or Complex Project, are all part of the A201 family of documents. They are used in the Design-Bid-Build delivery method.

See B101, Standard Form of Agreement Between Owner and Architect (with comments) for more information.

79. Answer: b and c

The standard of care in B101, Standard Form of Agreement Between Owner and Architect, means the architect needs to provide the care that is *ordinarily* provided by architects practicing under the same or similar circumstances. That also means the architect needs to provide an *average* standard of care and service to a client. This is also consistent with a common definition of standard of care.

This definition in B101 is very important, and can help an architect to protect herself in a litigation.

It is great to provide the highest standard of care and service to a client, but it is not mandated by B101. See B101, Standard Form of Agreement Between Owner and Architect (with comments) for more information.

80. Answer: c and f
Pay attention to the word "except."
Per B101, Standard Form of Agreement Between Owner and Architect, the owner does not need to provide either of the following, therefore they are the correct answers:
- certification from the owner's lender indicating that enough funds are available to pay for the design and construction of the project
- local zoning ordinances (This is part of the architect's scope of work.)

The owner does need to provide the following:
- a survey of the project site
- a program of the project
- testing required by the contract documents
- a soils report

81. Answer: b
Contract time uses calendar days, not actual working days. Therefore the target substantial completion date is May 29.

82. Answer: a
The consultant should be brought on board at the beginning of the project. The sooner they join the team, the better it will be for them to provide input. Pre-design stage is the correct answer.

83. Answer: a and b
The following consultants are typically placed under the owner's contract:
- survey engineer
- civil engineer

Placing the afore-mentioned consultants under the owner's contract will also substantially reduce the architect's liabilities. For example, if a survey engineer misses an easement on the survey plans and cause a huge extra cost for the project, the survey engineer and the owner, instead of the architect, will be responsible for the extra cost since the survey engineer is the owner's consultant.

The landscape architect can be placed in either the owner or architect contract.

The following consultants are typically placed under the architect's contract:
- structural engineer
- electrical engineer
- mechanical engineer
- plumbing engineer

B. Mock Exam Answers and Explanations: Case Study

84. Answer: a

Per A201, General Conditions of the Contract for Construction, the surveyor is typically hired by the owner.

85. Answer: a

Based on the site survey plan, the site is higher on the south, and slopes toward the north. This question is testing your ability to understand the contour lines on a site survey plan.

86. Answer: e and f

The surveyor and the party that hired the surveyor are responsible for the extra construction cost.

Per A201, General Conditions of the Contract for Construction, the owner shall furnish a survey describing physical characteristics, legal limitations, and utility locations for the project site. The surveyor is typically hired by the owner, but not always. Depending on the specific scope of the contract between the surveyor and the party that hired the surveyor, the surveyor may need to check not only the recorded easements with the county recorder's office, but also the easements shown on the city storm drain plan.

Some architects include a survey as part of their scope of work. This example shows the potential liabilities for this practice. In this case, if the surveyor is under the architect's contract, the owner will probably seek damages from both the architect and the surveyor.

87. Answer: b and d

The architect should educate the owner and try to convince him to accept the architect's suggestion. If the owner still does not want to accept the architect's suggestion, the architect should follow the owner's instruction and document the owner's rejection of the the suggestion.

Refusing to follow the owner's instruction and canceling the contract is not a very good choice. The architect can give the owner suggestions and advise, but the owner makes the ultimate decision.

Contacting the city and asking the city building official to assist the architect to convince the owner to accept the architect's suggestion will make the architect look weak, and the city building official normally does not get involved with these kinds of issues. This is a matter between the owner and the architect.

88. Answer: b
Buildable Areas = Lot Size - Easement Areas - Existing Areas with more than a 1 to 4 slope = 14,457 s.f. - 4,731 s.f. - 843 s.f. = 8,883 s.f.

40% of Buildable Areas = 3,553 s.f.

Actual Coverage = 2,725 s.f / 8,883 s.f. = 31% < 40% of buildable areas

89. Answer: c and d
Per AIA Document B101, Standard Form of Agreement Between Owner and Architect, failure of the owner to pay the architect per the agreement is a substantial nonperformance, and cause for termination or, at the architect's option, cause of suspension of performance of services under the agreement. If the architect elects to suspend services, the architect shall give seven-day written notice to the owner before doing so.

Being cool and just waiting until the owner has money to get paid will NOT help the architect get paid.

The architect has no right to stop the project.

Setting up a meeting with the owner to find common ground and arrange for a payment plan is unlikely to help the architect to get paid. This option will only encourage the owner not to pay or pay a smaller amount than he owes.

90. Answer: d
The conclusions and recommendations section of the geotechnical report will give the structural engineer information on footing and foundation design.
  * The site location and project development section normally includes a brief description of the site and the proposed project.
  * Field investigation includes information on test pits, etc.
  * Soils condition described the types and colors of soils, etc.

An architect should always compare the structural engineer's footing and foundation design against the recommentions of the geotechnical engineer. Some structural engineers just copy their standard notes and details and use them for many projects, and then fail to update them per the geotechnical report. It is also a good practice to list the geotechnical report information such as the title and date of the report, and contact information of the company that prepared the report.

91. Answer: a
At the construction document stage, civil plans typically require a submittal to a separate public works department. Architectural, structural plans, electrical, mechanical, and plumbing plans, as well as energy calculations, can all be submitted simultaneously to the building department.

92. Answer: a and b
The following should be included in the architect's feasibility studies:
- local zoning ordinances
- proposed design schedule

Recommendation for financing the project is not part of the architect's scope, and is not covered by architect's professional liabilities insurance. Recommendation for selecting the geotechnical and civil engineers is typically not included in the architect's feasibility studies either.

93. Answer: c
The least important questions the architect should ask is:
Does the building need to be sprinklered?
This question has the least impact on the planning and design of the building.

94. Answer: b and d
If the owner wants to expedite the project, he should choose the following delivery methods because they allow a portion of the design phase and construction phase overlap:
- design-build
- bridging

The following delivery methods will not shorten the overall project schedule:
- Bidding requires sufficient time for the contractors to review and bid the project.
- Hiring a construction manager as adviser may increase the overall project schedule. A construction manager acts as a third party, and may require extra time for his review.

95. Answer:
See the following table for the project tasks in the correct columns and project phase:

Project Phase	ArchiteG, Inc.	Smith and Associates
Pre-design	• design charrettes • coordination of geotechnical studies • development of overall project budget	• RFP responses
Design	• reviews and comments on progress plans	• outline specifications • selection of the mechanical systems • preparation of plans for permit
Construction	• evaluation of payment application	• organization of pre-proposal conference for subcontractors • review of shop drawings

C. How We Came Up with the Project Management (PjM) Mock Exam Questions

We came up with all the CE Mock Exam questions based on the ARE 5.0 Handbook, and we developed the Mock Exam based on the *four* weighted sections. See a detailed breakdown in the following tables:

Sections	Expected Number of Items	Actual Number of Items
Total	95	95
Section 1: Resource Management (7-13%)	6-12	7
• Determine criteria required to assemble team		3
• Assess criteria required to allocate and manage project resources (A/E)		4
Section 2: Project Work Planning (17-23%)	16-22	17
• Develop and maintain project work plan (U/A)		5
• Determine criteria required to develop and maintain project schedule (A/E)		5
• Determine appropriate communication to project team – owner, contractor, consultants and internal staff (U/A)		7
Section 3: Contracts (25-31%)	23-29	27
• Evaluate and verify adherence to owner/architect agreement (A/E)		9
• Interpret key elements of, and verify adherence to architect/consultant agreement (U/A)		6
• Interpret key elements of the owner/contractor agreement (U/A)		7
• Interpret key elements of the owner/consultant agreement to integrate the consultant's work into the project (U/A)		5
Section 4: Project Execution (17-23%)	16-22	21
• Evaluate compliance with construction budget (A/E)		4
• Evaluate and address changes in scope of work and scope creep (A/E)		3
• Evaluate project documentation to ensure it supports the specified delivery method (A/E)		6
• Identify and conform with the requirements set forth by authorities having jurisdiction in order to obtain approvals for the project (U/A)		8
Section 5: Project Quality Control (19-25%)	18-23	23
• Apply procedures required for adherence to laws and regulations relating to the project (U/A)		8
• Identify steps in maintaining project quality control, and reducing risks and liabilities (A/E)		5
• Perform quality control reviews of project documentation throughout life of project (A/E)		5
• Evaluate management of the design process to maintain integrity of design objectives (A/E)		5

Note: If the text on following tables is too small for you to read, then you can go to our forum, sign up for a free account, and download the FREE full-size jpeg format files for these tables at GeeForum.com

Appendixes

A. List of Figures

B. Official reference materials suggested by NCARB

1. Resources Available While Testing
Tips:
- *You need to read through these pages several times and become very familiar with them to save time in the real ARE exams.*

United States. American Institute of Steel Construction, Inc. *Steel Construction Manual*; 14th edition. Chicago, Illinois, 2011.

Beam Diagrams and Formulas:
- Simple Beam: Diagrams and Formulas - Conditions 1-3, page 3-213; Conditions 4-6, page 3-214; Conditions 7-9, page 3-215
- Beam Fixed at Both Ends: Diagrams and Formulas - Conditions 15-17, page 3-218
- Beam Overhanging One Support: Diagrams and Formulas - Conditions 24-28, pages 3-221 & 222

Dimensions and Properties:
- W Shapes 44 thru 27: Dimensions and Properties, pages 1-12 thru 17
- W Shapes 24 thru W14x145: Dimensions and Properties, pages 1-18 thru 23
- W Shapes 14x132 thru W4: Dimensions and Properties, pages 1-24 thru 29
- C Shapes: Dimensions and Properties, pages 1-36 & 37
- Angles: Properties, pages 1-42 thru 49
- Rectangular HSS: Dimensions and Properties, pages 1-74 thru 91
- Square HSS: Dimensions and Properties, pages 1-92 thru 95
- Round HSS: Dimensions and Properties, pages 1-96 thru 100

United States. International Code Council, Inc. *2012 International Building Code.* Country Club Hills, Illinois, 2011.

Live and Concentrated Loads:
- Uniform and Concentrated Loads: IBC Table 1607.1, pages 340-341

2. Typical Beam Nomenclature

The following typical beam nomenclature is excerpted from:
United States. American Institute of Steel Construction, Inc. *Steel Construction Manual*; 14th edition. Chicago, Illinois, 2011.

E	Modulus of Elasticity of steel at 29,000 ksi	V_2	Vertical shear at right reaction point, or to left of intermediate reaction of beam, kips
I	Moment of Inertia of beam, in^4	V_3	Vertical shear at right reaction point, or to right of intermediate reaction of beam, kips
L	Total length of beam between reaction point, ft	V_x	Vertical shear at distance x from end of beam, kips
M_{max}	Maximum moment, kip-in	W	Total load on beam, kips
M_1	Maximum moment in left section of beam, kip-in	A	Measured distance along beam, in
M_2	Maximum moment in right section of beam, kip-in	B	Measured distance along beam which may be greater or less than a, in
M_3	Maximum positive moment in beam with combined end moment conditions, kip-in	L	Total length of beam between reaction points, in
M_x	Maximum at distance x from end of beam, kip-in	W	Uniformly distributed load per unit of length, kips/in
P	Concentrated load, kips	w_1	Uniformly distributed load per unit of length nearest left reaction, kips/in
P_1	Concentrated load nearest left reaction, kips	w_2	Uniformly distributed load per unit of length nearest right reaction and of different magnitude than w1, kips/in
P_2	Concentrated load nearest right reaction and of different magnitude than P_1, kips	X	Any distance measured along beam from left reaction, in
R	End beam reaction for any condition of symmetrical loading, kips	x_1	Any distance measured along overhang section of beam from nearest reaction point, in
R_1	Left end beam reaction, kips	Δ_{max}	Maximum deflection, in
R_2	Right end or intermediate beam reaction, kips	Δa	Deflection at point of load, in
R_3	Right end beam reaction, kips	Δx	Deflection at point x distance from left reaction, in
V	Maximum vertical shear for any condition of symmetrical loading, kips	Δx_1	Deflection of overhang section of beam at any distance from nearest reaction point, in
V_1	Maximum vertical shear in left section of beam, kips		

3. Formulas Available While Testing

Tips:

- *These formulas and references will be available during the real exam. You should read through them a few times before the exam to become familiar with them. This will save you a lot of time during the real exam, and will help you solve structural calculations and other problems.*

Structural:

Flexural stress at extreme fiber

$$f = \frac{Mc}{I} = \frac{M}{S}$$

Flexural stress at any fiber

$$f = \frac{My}{I}$$

where y = distance from neutral axis to fiber

Average vertical shear

$$v = \frac{V}{A} = \frac{V}{dt}$$

for beams and girders

Horizontal shearing stress at any section A-A

$$v = \frac{VQ}{Ib}$$

where Q = statical moment about the neutral axis of the entire section of that portion of the cross-section lying outside of section A-A

b = width at section A-A

Electrical

$$Foot - candles = \frac{lumens}{area\ in\ ft^2}$$

$$Foot - candles = \frac{(lamp\ lumens)\ x\ (lamps\ per\ fixture)\ x\ (number\ of\ fixtures)\ x\ (CU)\ x\ (LLF)}{area\ in\ ft^2}$$

$$Number\ of\ luminaires = \frac{(foot - candles)\ x\ (floor\ area)}{(lumens)\ x\ (CU)\ x\ (LLF)}$$

where CU = coefficient of utilization

LLF = Light Loss Factor

$$DF_{AV} = 0.2x \frac{window\ area}{floor\ area}$$
for spaces with sidelighting or toplighting with vertical monitors

watts = volts x amperes x power factor
for AC circuits only

Demand charge = maximum power demand x demand tariff

Plumbing
$$1\ psi = 2.31\ feet\ of\ water$$

$$1\ cubic\ foot = 7.5\ U.S.\ gallons$$

HVAC

$$\frac{BTU}{year} = peak\ heat\ loss\ x\ \frac{full-load\ hours}{year}$$

$$BTU/h = (cfm)\ x\ (1.08)\ x\ (\varDelta T)$$

$$1\ kWh = 3,400\ BTU/h$$

$$1\ ton\ of\ air\ conditioning = 12,000\ BTU/h$$

$$BTU/h = (U)\ x\ (A)\ x\ (T_d)$$ *where Td is the difference between indoor and outdoor temperatures*

$$U = 1/R_t$$

$$U_o = \frac{(U_w \times A_w) + (U_{op} \times A_{op})}{Ao}$$
where o = total wall, w = window, and op = opaque wall

$$U_o = \frac{(U_R \times A_R) + (U_S \times A_S)}{Ao}$$

where o = total roof, R = roof, and S = skylight

$$R = x/k$$

where x = thickness of material in inches

$$Heat\ required = \frac{BTU/h}{temperature\ differential} \times (24\ hours) \times (DD\ °F)$$

where DD = degree days

Acoustics

$$\lambda = \frac{c}{f}$$

where λ = wavelength of sound (ft)
c = velocity of sound (fps)
f = frequency of sound (Hz)

$$a = SAC\ x\ S$$

where a = Absorption of a material used in space (sabins)
SAC = Sound Absorption Coefficient of the material
S = Exposed surface area of the material (ft ^{2})

$$A = \Sigma a$$

Where A = Total sound absorption of a room (sabins)
$\Sigma a = (S_1\ x\ SAC_1) + (S_2\ x\ SAC_2) + \ldots$

$$T = 0.05 \times \frac{V}{A}$$

where T = Reverberation time (seconds)
V = Volume of space (ft ^{3})

$$NRC = average\ SAC\ for\ frequency\ bands\ 250, 500, 1000, and\ 2000\ Hz$$

4. Common Abbreviations

Tips:

- *You need to read through these common abbreviations several times and become very familiar with them to save time in the real ARE exams.*

Professional Organizations, Societies, and Agencies

American Concrete Institute	ACI
American Institute of Architects	AIA
American Institute of Steel Construction	AISC
American National Standards Institute	ANSI
American Society for Testing and Materials	ASTM
American Society of Civil Engineers	ASCE
American Society of Heating, Refrigerating, and Air-Conditioning Engineers	ASHRAE
American Society of Mechanical Engineers	ASME
American Society of Plumbing Engineers	ASPE
Architectural Woodwork Institute	AWI
Construction Specifications Institute	CSI
Department of Housing and Urban Development	HUD
Environmental Protection Agency	EPA
Federal Emergency Management Agency	FEMA
National Fire Protection Association	NFPA
Occupational Safety and Health Administration	OSHA
U.S. Green Building Council	USGBC

Tips:

- *You need to look through the following codes and regulations & AIA contract documents several times and become very familiar with them to save time in the real ARE exams. Read some of the important sections in details.*

AIA Contract Documents

A101-2007, Standard Form of Agreement Between Owner and Contractor - Stipulated Sum	A101
A201-2007, General Conditions of the Contract for Construction	A201
A305-1986, Contractor's Qualification Statement	A305
A701-1997, Instructions to Bidders	A701
B101-2007, Standard Form of Agreement Between Owner and Architect	B101
C401-2007, Standard Form of Agreement Between Architect and Consultant	C401
G701-2001, Change Order	G701
G702-1992, Application and Certificate for Payment	G702
G703-1992, Continuation Sheet	G703
G704-2000, Certificate of Substantial Completion	G704

Codes and Regulations

ADA Standards for Accessible Design	ADA

International Code Council	ICC
International Building Code	IBC
International Energy Conservation Code	IECC
International Existing Building Code	IEBC
International Mechanical Code	IMC
International Plumbing Code	IPC
International Residential Code	IRC
Leadership in Energy and Environmental Design	LEED
National Electrical Code	NEC

Commonly Used Terms

Air Handling Unit	AHU
Authority Having Jurisdiction	AHJ
Building Information Modeling	BIM
Concrete Masonry Unit	CMU
Contract Administration	CA
Construction Document	CD
Dead Load	DL
Design Development	DD
Exterior Insulation and Finish System	EIFS
Furniture, Furnishings & Equipment	FF&E
Floor Area Ratio	FAR
Heating, Ventilating, and Air Conditioning	HVAC
Insulating Glass Unit	IGU
Indoor Air Quality	IAQ
Indoor Environmental Quality	IEQ
Live Load	LL
Material Safety Data Sheets	MSDS
Photovoltaic	PV
Reflected Ceiling Plan	RCP
Schematic Design	SD
Variable Air Volume	VAV
Volatile Organic Compound	VOC
British Thermal Unit	btu
Cubic Feet per Minute	cfm
Cubic Feet per Second	cfs
Cubic Foot	cu. ft. ft^3
Cubic Inch	cu. in. in^3
Cubic Yard	cu. yd. yd^3
Decibel	dB
Foot	ft
Foot-candle	fc
Gross Square Feet	gsf

Impact Insulation Class	IIC
Inch	in
Net Square Feet	nsf
Noise Reduction Coefficient	NRC
Pound	lb
Pounds per Linear Foot	plf
Pounds per Square Foot	psf
Pounds per Square Inch	psi
Sound Transmission Class	STC
Square Foot	sq. ft.
	sf
	ft^2
Square Inch	sq. in.
	in^2
Square Yard	sq. yd.

5. General NCARB reference materials for ARE:

Per NCARB, all candidates should become familiar with the latest version of the following codes:

International Code Council, Inc. (ICC)
International Building Code
International Mechanical Code
International Plumbing Code

National Fire Protection Association (NFPA)
Life Safety Code (NFPA 101)
National Electrical Code (NFPA 70)

National Research Council of Canada
National Building Code of Canada
National Plumbing Code of Canada
National Fire Code of Canada

American Institute of Architects
AIA Documents

6. Official NCARB reference materials matrix

Per NCARB, all candidates should become familiar with the latest version of the following:

Reference	PcM	PjM	PA	PPD	PDD	CE
ADA Standards for Accessible Design U.S. Department of Justice, Latest Edition			■	■		
Code of Ethics and Professional Conduct AIA Office of General Counsel. The American Institute of Architects, latest edition	■					
The Architect's Handbook of Professional Practice The American Institute of Architects John Wiley & Sons, latest edition	■	■	■	■	■	■
The Architect's Studio Companion: Rules of Thumb for Preliminary Design Edward Allen and Joseph Iano John Wiley & Sons, 6th edition, 2017			■	■		
Architectural Acoustics. M. David Egan. J. Ross Publishing. Reprint. Original publication McGraw Hill, latest edition				■		
Architectural Graphic Standards The American Institute of Architects John Wiley & Sons, latest edition			■	■		
Building Codes Illustrated: A Guide to Understanding the International Building Code. Francis D.K. Ching and Steven R. Winkel, FAIA, PE. John Wiley & Sons, latest edition			■	■		
Building Construction Illustrated Francis D. K. Ching John Wiley & Sons, latest edition			■	■		
Building Structures James Ambrose and Patrick Tripeny John Wiley & Sons, 3rd edition, Latest Edition				■	■	
CSI MasterFormat. The Construction Specifications Institute, latest edition					■	■
Daylighting Handbook I Christoph Reinhart Building Technology Press, latest edition			■	■		
Dictionary of Architecture and Construction. Cyril M. Harris. McGraw-Hill, Latest edition			■	■	■	
Framework for Design Excellence American Institute of Architects Available Online			■	■		

Reference	PcM	PjM	PA	PPD	PDD	CE
Fundamentals of Building Construction: Materials and Methods Edward Allen and Joseph Iano John Wiley & Sons, latest edition				X	X	
Green Building Illustrated Francis D.K. Ching and Ian M. Shapiro Wiley, latest edition				X	X	
The Green Studio Handbook: Environmental Strategies for Schematic Design Alison G. Kwok and Walter Grondzik Routledge, latest edition			X	X		
Heating, Cooling, Lighting: Sustainable Design Methods for Architects. Norbert Lechner. John Wiley & Sons, latest edition				X	X	
The HOK Guidebook to Sustainable Design Sandra F. Mendler, William Odell, and Mary Ann Lazarus John Wiley & Sons, latest edition			X	X	X	
ICC A117.1-2009 Accessible and Usable Buildings and Facilities International Code Council, 2010			X	X	X	
International Building Code International Code Council, latest edition			X	X	X	
Law for Architects: What You Need to Know. Robert F. Herrmann and the Attorneys at Menaker & Herrmann LLP. W. W. Norton, latest edition	X					
Legislative Guidelines and Model Law/Model Regulations National Council of Architectural Registration Boards, latest edition	X					
Mechanical & Electrical Equipment for Buildings. Walter T. Grondzik, Alison G. Kwok, Benjamin Stein, and John S. Reynolds, Editors. John Wiley & Sons, latest edition				X	X	
Mechanical and Electrical Systems in Buildings. Richard R. Janis and William K. Y. Tao. Prentice Hall, latest edition				X	X	
Model Rules of Conduct National Council of Architectural Registration Boards, latest edition	X					

Reference	PcM	PjM	PA	PPD	PDD	CE
Olin's Construction Principles, Materials, and Methods. H. Leslie Simmons. John Wiley & Sons, latest edition				■	■	
Planning and Urban Design Standards American Planning Association John Wiley & Sons, latest edition			■	■		
Plumbing, Electricity, Acoustics: Sustainable Design Methods for Architecture. Norbert Lechner. John Wiley & Sons, latest edition				■	■	
Problem Seeking: An Architectural Programming Primer William M. Peña and Steven A. Parshall John Wiley & Sons, latest edition			■			
Professional Practice: A Guide to Turning Designs into Buildings. Paul Segal, FAIA. W. W. Norton, latest edition	■	■	■			
The Professional Practice of Architectural Working Drawings. Osamu A. Wakita, Nagy R. Bakhoum, and Richard M. Linde. John Wiley & Sons, latest edition				■	■	
The Project Resource Manual: CSI Manual of Practice. The Construction Specifications Institute. McGraw-Hill, latest edition		■			■	■
Simplified Engineering for Architects and Builders James Ambrose and Patrick Tripeny John Wiley & Sons, latest edition				■	■	
Site Planning and Design Handbook Thomas H. Russ McGraw-Hill, latest edition			■	■		
Space Planning Basics Mark Karlen and Rob Fleming John Wiley & Sons, latest edition			■			
Steel Construction Manual American Institute of Steel Construction Ingram, latest edition					■	
Structural Design: A Practical Guide for Architects James R. Underwood and Michele Chiuini John Wiley & Sons, latest edition				■	■	
Structures Daniel Schodek and Martin Bechthold Pearson/Prentice Hall, latest edition						

Reference	PcM	PjM	PA	PPD	PDD	CE
Sun, Wind, and Light: Architectural Design Strategies G.Z. Brown and Mark DeKay John Wiley & Sons, latest edition			■	■		
Sustainable Construction: Green Building Design and Delivery Charles J. Kibert. John Wiley & Sons, latest edition				■		
A Visual Dictionary of Architecture Francis D.K. Ching John Wiley & Sons, latest edition				■	■	

The following AIA Contract Documents have content covered in the of ARE 5.0 exams. Candidates can access them for free through their NCARB Record.

Document	PcM	PjM	PA	PPD	PDD	CE
A101-2017, Standard Form of Agreement Between Owner and Contractor where the basis of payment is a Stipulated Sum		■				■
A133-2019, Standard Form of Agreement Between Owner and Construction Manager as Constructor where the basis of payment is the Cost of the Work Plus a Fee with a Guaranteed Maximum Price		■				
A195-2008, Standard Form of Agreement Between Owner and Contractor for Integrated Project Delivery		■				
A201-2017, General Conditions of the Contract for Construction		■				■
A295-2008, General Conditions of the Contract for Integrated Project Delivery		■				
A305-1986, Contractor's Qualification Statement						■
A701-2018, Instructions to Bidders						■
B101-2017, Standard Form of Agreement Between Owner and Architect	■	■				
B195-2008, Standard Form of Agreement Between Owner and Architect for Integrated Project Delivery		■				
C401-2017, Standard Form of Agreement Between Architect and Consultant	■					■

Document	PcM	PjM	PA	PPD	PDD	CE
G701-2017, Change Order						
G702-1992, Application and Certificate for Payment						
G703-1992, Continuation Sheet						
G704-2017, Certificate of Substantial Completion						

The following are some extra study materials if you have some additional time and want to learn more. If you are tight on time, you can simply look through them and focus on the sections that cover your weakness:

ACI Code 318-05 (Building Code Requirements for Reinforced Concrete)
American Concrete Institute, 2005

OR
CAN/CSA-A23.1-94 (Concrete Materials and Methods of Concrete Construction) and CAN/CSA-A23.3-94 (Design of Concrete Structures for Buildings)
Canadian Standards Association

Design Value for Wood Construction
American Wood Council, 2005

Elementary Structures for Architects and Builders, Fourth Edition
Ronald E. Shaeffer
Prentice Hall, 2006

Introduction to Wood Design
Canadian Wood Council, 2005

Manual of Steel Construction: Allowable Stress Design; 9th Edition.
American Institute of Steel Construction, Inc. Chicago, Illinois, 1989

National Building Code of Canada, 2005
Parts 1, 3, 4, 9; Appendix A
Supplement
Chapters 1, 2, 4; Commentaries A, D, F, H, I

NEHRP (National Earthquake Hazards Reduction Program) Recommended Provisions for Seismic Regulations for New Buildings and Other Structures Parts 1 and 2
FEMA 2003

Simplified Building Design for Wind and Earthquake Forces
James Ambrose and Dimitry Vergun
John Wiley & Sons, 1997

Simplified Design of Concrete Structures,
Eighth Edition
James Ambrose, Patrick Tripeny
John Wiley & Sons, 2007

Simplified Design of Masonry Structures
James Ambrose
John Wiley & Sons, 1997

Simplified Design of Steel Structures, Eighth Edition
James Ambrose, Patrick Tripeny
John Wiley & Sons, 2007

Simplified Design of Wood Structures, Fifth Edition
James Ambrose
John Wiley & Sons, 2009

Simplified Mechanics and Strength of Materials, Fifth Edition
Harry Parker and James Ambrose
John Wiley & Sons, 2002

Standard Specifications Load Tables &Weight Tables for Steel Joists and Joist Girders
Steel Joist Institute, latest edition

Steel Construction Manual, Latest edition
American Institute of Steel Construction, 2006

OR
Handbook of Steel Construction, Latest edition; and *CAN/CSA-S16-01 and CISC Commentary*
Canadian Institute of Steel Construction

Steel Deck Institute Tables
Steel Deck Institute

OR
LSD Steel Deck Tables
Caradon Metal Building Products

Structural Concepts and Systems for Architects and Engineers, Second Edition
T.Y. Lin and Sidney D. Stotesbury
Van Nostrand Reinhold, 1988

Structural Design: A Practical Guide for Architects
James Underwood and Michele Chiuini
John Wiley & Sons, latest edition

Structure in Architecture: The Building of Buildings
Mario Salvadori with Robert Heller
Prentice-Hall, 1986

Understanding Structures
Fuller Moore
McGraw-Hill, 1999

Wood Design Manual and *CAN/CSA-086.1-94 and Commentary*
Canadian Wood Council

C. Other reference materials

Chen, Gang. *Building Construction: Project Management, Construction Administration, Drawings, Specs, Detailing Tips, Schedules, Checklists, and Secrets Others Don't Tell You (Architectural Practice Simplified, 2nd edition)*. ArchiteG, Inc., A good introduction to the architectural practice and construction documents and service, including discussions of MasterSpec format and specification sections.

Chen, Gang. ***LEED v4 Green Associate Exam Guide (LEED GA):*** *Comprehensive Study Materials, Sample Questions, Mock Exam, Green Building LEED Certification, and Sustainability*, Book 2, LEED Exam Guide series, ArchiteG.com, the latest edition. ArchiteG, Inc. Latest Edition. This is a very comprehensive and concise book on the LEED Green Associate Exam. Some readers have passed the LEED Green Associate Exam by studying this book for 10 hours.

Ching, Francis. *Architecture: Form, Space, & Order*. Wiley, latest edition. It is one of the best architectural books that you can have. I still flip through it every now and then. It is a great book for inspiration.

Frampton, Kenneth. *Modern Architecture: A Critical History*. Thames and Hudson, London, latest edition. A valuable resource for architectural history.

Jarzombek, Mark M. (Author), Vikramaditya Prakash (Author), Francis D. K. Ching (Editor). *A Global History of Architecture*. Wiley, latest edition. A valuable and comprehensive resource for architectural history with 1000 b & w photos, 50 color photos, and 1500 b & w illustrations. It doesn't limit the topic on a Western perspective, but rather through a global vision.

Trachtenberg, Marvin and Isabelle Hyman. *Architecture: From Pre-history to Post-Modernism*. Prentice Hall, Englewood Cliffs, NJ latest edition. A valuable and comprehensive resource for architectural history.

D. Some Important Information about Architects and the Profession of Architecture

What Architects Do?

Architects plan and design houses, factories, office buildings, and other structures.

Duties

Architects typically do the following:

- meet with clients to determine objectives and requirements for structures
- give preliminary estimates on cost and construction time
- prepare structure specifications
- direct workers who prepare drawings and documents
- prepare scaled drawings, either with computer software or by hand
- prepare contract documents for building contractors
- manage construction contracts
- visit worksites to ensure that construction adheres to architectural plans
- seek new work by marketing and giving presentations

People need places to live, work, play, learn, shop, and eat. Architects are responsible for designing these places. They work on public or private projects and design both indoor and outdoor spaces. Architects can be commissioned to design anything from a single room to an entire complex of buildings.

Architects discuss the objectives, requirements, and budget of a project with clients. In some cases, architects provide various predesign services, such as feasibility and environmental impact studies, site selection, cost analyses, and design requirements.

Architects develop final construction plans after discussing and agreeing on the initial proposal with clients. These plans show the building's appearance and details of its construction. Accompanying these plans are drawings of the structural system; air-conditioning, heating, and ventilating systems; electrical systems; communications systems; and plumbing. Sometimes, landscape plans are included as well. In developing designs, architects must follow state and local building codes, zoning laws, fire regulations, and other ordinances, such as those requiring easy access to buildings for people who are disabled.

Computer-aided design and drafting (CADD) and building information modeling (BIM) have replaced traditional drafting paper and pencil as the most common methods for creating designs and construction drawings. However, hand-drawing skills are still required, especially during the conceptual stages of a project and when an architect is at a construction site.

As construction continues, architects may visit building sites to ensure that contractors follow the design, adhere to the schedule, use the specified materials, and meet work-quality standards. The job is not complete until all construction is finished, required tests are conducted, and construction costs are paid.

Architects may also help clients get construction bids, select contractors, and negotiate construction contracts.

Architects often collaborate with workers in related occupations, such as civil engineers, urban and regional planners, drafters, interior designers, and landscape architects.

Work Environment

Although architects usually work in an office, they must also travel to construction sites.

Architects held about 128,800 jobs in 2016. The largest employers of architects were as follows:

Architectural, engineering, and related services	68%
Self-employed workers	20%
Government	3%
Construction	2%

Architects spend much of their time in offices, where they meet with clients, develop reports and drawings, and work with other architects and engineers. They also visit construction sites to ensure clients' objectives are met and to review the progress of projects. Some architects work from home offices.

Work Schedules

Most architects work full time and many work additional hours, especially when facing deadlines. Self-employed architects may have more flexible work schedules.

How to Become an Architect

There are typically three main steps to becoming a licensed architect: completing a professional degree in architecture, gaining relevant experience through a paid internship, and passing the Architect Registration Examination.

Education

In all states, earning a professional degree in architecture is typically the first step to becoming an architect. Most architects earn their professional degree through a five-year Bachelor of Architecture degree program, intended for students with no previous architectural training. Many earn a master's degree in architecture, which can take one to five years in addition to the time spent earning a bachelor's degree. The amount of time required depends on the extent of the student's previous education and training in architecture.

A typical bachelor's degree program includes courses in architectural history and theory, building design with an emphasis on computer-aided design and drafting (CADD), structures, construction methods, professional practices, math, physical sciences, and liberal arts. Central to most architectural programs is the design studio, where students apply the skills and concepts learned in the classroom to create drawings and three-dimensional models of their designs.

Currently, thirty-four states require that architects hold a professional degree in architecture from one of the 123 schools of architecture accredited by the National Architectural Accrediting Board (NAAB). State licensing requirements can be found at the National Council of Architectural

Registration Boards (NCARB). In the states that do not have that requirement, applicants can become licensed with eight to thirteen years of related work experience in addition to a high school diploma. However, most architects in these states still obtain a professional degree in architecture.

Training

All state architectural registration boards require architecture graduates to complete a lengthy paid internship—generally three years of experience—before they may sit for the Architect Registration Examination. Most new graduates complete their training period by working at architectural firms through the Architectural Experience Program (AXP), a program run by NCARB that guides students through the internship process. Some states allow a portion of the training to occur in the offices of employers in related careers, such as engineers and general contractors. Architecture students who complete internships while still in school can count some of that time toward the three-year training period.

Interns in architectural firms may help design part of a project. They may help prepare architectural documents and drawings, build models, and prepare construction drawings on CADD. Interns may also research building codes and write specifications for building materials, installation criteria, the quality of finishes, and other related details. Licensed architects will take the documents that interns produce, make edits to them, finalize plans, and then sign and seal the documents.

Licenses, Certifications, and Registrations

All states and the District of Columbia require architects to be licensed. Licensing requirements typically include completing a professional degree in architecture, gaining relevant experience through a paid internship, and passing the Architect Registration Examination.

Most states also require some form of continuing education to keep a license, and some additional states are expected to adopt mandatory continuing education. Requirements vary by state but usually involve additional education through workshops, university classes, conferences, self-study courses, or other sources.

A growing number of architects voluntarily seek certification from NCARB. This certification makes it easier to become licensed in other states, because it is the primary requirement for reciprocity of licensing among state boards that are NCARB members. In 2014, approximately one-third of all licensed architects had the certification.

Advancement

After many years of work experience, some architects advance to become architectural and engineering managers. These managers typically coordinate the activities of employees and may work on larger construction projects.

Important Qualities

Analytical skills. Architects must understand the content of designs and the context in which they were created. For example, architects must understand the locations of mechanical systems and how those systems affect building operations.

Communication skills. Architects share their ideas, both in oral presentations and in writing, with clients, other architects, and workers who help prepare drawings. Many also give presentations to explain their ideas and designs.

Creativity. Architects design the overall look of houses, buildings, and other structures. Therefore, the final product should be attractive and functional.

Organizational skills. Architects often manage contracts. Therefore, they must keep records related to the details of a project, including total cost, materials used, and progress.

Technical skills. Architects need to use CADD technology to create plans as part of building information modeling (BIM).

Visualization skills. Architects must be able to see how the parts of a structure relate to each other. They also must be able to visualize how the overall building will look once completed.

Pay

The median annual wage for architects was $79,380 in May 2018. The median wage is the wage at which half the workers in an occupation earned more than that amount and half earned less. The lowest 10 percent earned less than $48,020, and the highest ten percent earned more than $138,120.

In May 2018, the median annual wages for architects in the top industries in which they worked were as follows:

Government	$92,940
Architectural, engineering, and related services	$78,460
Construction	$78,110

Most architects work full time and many work additional hours, especially when facing deadlines. Self-employed architects may have more flexible work hours.

Job Outlook

Employment of architects is projected to grow 4 percent from 2016 to 2026, slower than the average for all occupations.

Architects will be needed to make plans and designs for the construction and renovation of homes, offices, retail stores, and other structures. Many school districts and universities are expected to build new facilities or renovate existing ones. In addition, demand is expected for more healthcare facilities as the baby-boomer population ages and as more individuals use healthcare services. The construction of new retail establishments may also require more architects.

Demand is projected for architects with a knowledge of "green design," also called sustainable design. Sustainable design emphasizes the efficient use of resources, such as energy and water conservation; waste and pollution reduction; and environmentally friendly design, specifications, and materials. Rising energy costs and increased concern about the environment have led to many new buildings being built with more sustainable designs.

The use of CADD and, more recently, BIM, has made architects more productive. These technologies have allowed architects to do more work without the help of drafters while making it easier to share the work with engineers, contractors, and clients.

Job Prospects

With a high number of students graduating with degrees in architecture, very strong competition for internships and jobs is expected. Competition for jobs will be especially strong at the most prestigious architectural firms. Those with up-to-date technical skills—including a strong grasp of CADD and BIM—and experience in sustainable design will have an advantage.

Employment of architects is strongly tied to the activity of the construction industry. Therefore, these workers may experience periods of unemployment when there is a slowdown in requests for new projects or when the overall level of construction falls.

State & Area Data
Occupational Employment Statistics (OES)

The Occupational Employment Statistics (OES) program produces employment and wage estimates annually for over 800 occupations. These estimates are available for the nation as a whole, for individual states, and for metropolitan and nonmetropolitan areas. The link below goes to OES data maps for employment and wages by state and area.
https://www.bls.gov/oes/current/oes171011.htm#st

Projections Central

Occupational employment projections are developed for all states by Labor Market Information (LMI) or individual state Employment Projections offices. All state projections data are available at www.projectionscentral.com. Information on this site allows projected employment growth for an occupation to be compared among states or to be compared within one state. In addition, states may produce projections for areas; there are links to each state's websites where these data may be retrieved.

CareerOneStop

CareerOneStop includes hundreds of occupational profiles with data available by state and metro area. There are links in the left-hand side menu to compare occupational employment by state and occupational wages by local area or metro area. There is also a salary info tool to search for wages by zip code.

Related Occupations

Architects design buildings and related structures. Construction managers, like architects, also plan and coordinate activities concerned with the construction and maintenance of buildings and facilities. Others who engage in similar work are landscape architects, civil engineers, urban and regional planners, and designers, including interior designers, commercial and industrial designers, and graphic designers.

Sources of Additional Information

Disclaimer:
Links to non-BLS Internet sites are provided for your convenience and do not constitute an endorsement.

Information about education and careers in architecture can be obtained from:
- The American Institute of Architects, 1735 New York Ave. NW., Washington, DC 20006. Internet: http://www.aia.org
- National Architectural Accrediting Board: http://www.naab.org/
- National Council of Architectural Registration Boards, Suite 1100K, 1801 K St. NW., Washington, D.C. 20006. Internet: http://www.ncarb.org
  OOH ONET Codes 17-1011.00"

Source: Bureau of Labor Statistics, U.S. Department of Labor, *Occupational Outlook Handbook*, Architects, on the Internet at https://www.bls.gov/ooh/architecture-and-engineering/architects.htm (visited June 06, 2019).

Last Modified Date: Friday, April 12, 2019

Note:
Please check the website above for the latest information.

E. AIA Compensation Survey

Every 3 years, AIA publishes a Compensation Survey for various positions at architectural firms across the country. It is a good idea to find out the salary before you make the final decision to become an architect. If you are already an architect, it is also a good idea to determine if you are underpaid or overpaid.

See following link for some sample pages for the latest AIA Compensation Survey:

https://www.aia.org/resources/8066-aia-compensation-report

F. So ... You would Like to Study Architecture

To study architecture, you need to learn how to draft, how to understand and organize spaces and the interactions between interior and exterior spaces, how to do design, and how to communicate effectively. You also need to understand the history of architecture.

As an architect, a leader for a team of various design professionals, you not only need to know architecture, but also need to understand enough of your consultants' work to be able to coordinate them. Your consultants include soils and civil engineers, landscape architects, structural, electrical, mechanical, and plumbing engineers, interior designers, sign consultants, etc.

There are two major career paths for you in architecture: practice as an architect or teach in colleges or universities. The earlier you determine which path you are going to take, the more likely you will be successful at an early age. Some famous and well-respected architects, like my USC alumnus Frank Gehry, have combined the two paths successfully. They teach at the universities and have their own architectural practice. Even as a college or university professor, people respect you more if you have actual working experience and have some built projects. If you only teach in colleges or universities but have no actual working experience and have no built projects, people will consider you as a "paper" architect, and they are not likely to take you seriously, because they will think you probably do not know how to put a real building together.

In the U.S., if you want to practice architecture, you need to obtain an architect's license. It requires a combination of passing scores on the Architectural Registration Exam (ARE) and 8 years of education and/or qualified working experience, including at least 1 year of working experience in the U.S. Your working experience needs to be under the supervision of a licensed architect to be counted as qualified working experience for your architect's license.

If you work for a landscape architect or civil engineer or structural engineer, some states' architectural licensing boards will count your experience at a discounted rate for the qualification of your architect's license. For example, 2 years of experience working for a civil engineer may be counted as 1 year of qualified experience for your architect's license. You need to contact your state's architectural licensing board for specific licensing requirements for your state.

If you want to teach in colleges or universities, you probably want to obtain a master's degree or a Ph.D. It is not very common for people in the architectural field to have a Ph.D. One reason is that there are few Ph.D. programs for architecture. Another reason is that architecture is considered a profession and requires a license. Many people think an architect's license is more important than a Ph.D. degree. In many states, you need to have an architect's license to even use the title "architect," or the terms "architectural" or "architecture" to advertise your service. You cannot call yourself an architect if you do not have an architect's license, even if you have a Ph.D. in architecture. Violation of these rules brings punishment.

To become a tenured professor, you need to have a certain number of publications and pass the evaluation for the tenure position. Publications are very important for tenure track positions. Some people say for the tenured track positions in universities and colleges, it is "publish or perish."

The American Institute of Architects (AIA) is the national organization for the architectural profession. Membership is voluntary. There are different levels of AIA membership. Only licensed architects can be (full) AIA members. If you are an architectural student or an intern but not a licensed architect yet, you can join as an associate AIA member. Contact AIA for detailed information.

The National Council of Architectural Registration Boards (NCARB) is a nonprofit federation of architectural licensing boards. It has some very useful programs, such as IDP, to assist you in obtaining your architect's license. Contact NCARB for detailed information.

Back Page Promotion

You may be interested in some other books written by Gang Chen:

A. **ARE Mock Exam series & ARE Exam Guide series.** See the following link:
   http://www.GreenExamEducation.com

B. **LEED Exam Guides series.** See the following link:
   http://www.GreenExamEducation.com

C. ***Building Construction:*** *Project Management, Construction Administration, Drawings, Specs, Detailing Tips, Schedules, Checklists, and Secrets Others Don't Tell You (Architectural Practice Simplified, 2nd edition)*
   http://www.GreenExamEducation.com

D. ***Planting Design Illustrated***
   http://www.GreenExamEducation.com

ARE Mock Exam Series & ARE Exam Guide Series

ARE 5.0 Mock Exam Series

Practice Management (PcM) ARE 5.0 Mock Exam (Architect Registration Examination): ARE 5.0 Overview, Exam Prep Tips, Hotspots, Case Studies, Drag-and-Place, Solutions and Explanations. **ISBN**: 9781612650388

Project Management (PjM) ARE 5.0 Mock Exam (Architect Registration Examination): ARE 5.0 Overview, Exam Prep Tips, Hotspots, Case Studies, Drag-and-Place, Solutions and Explanations. **ISBN**: 9781612650371

Programming & Analysis (PA) ARE 5.0 Mock Exam (Architect Registration Exam): ARE 5.0 Overview, Exam Prep Tips, Hotspots, Case Studies, Drag-and-Place, Solutions and Explanations. **ISBN**: 9781612650326

Project Planning & Design (PPD) ARE 5.0 Mock Exam (Architect Registration Examination): ARE 5.0 Overview, Exam Prep Tips, Hotspots, Case Studies, Drag-and-Place, Solutions and Explanations. **ISBN**: 9781612650296

Project Development & Documentation (PDD) ARE 5.0 Mock Exam (Architect Registration Examination): ARE 5.0 Overview, Exam Prep Tips, Hotspots, Case Studies, Drag-and-Place, Solutions and Explanations
ISBN: 9781612650258

Construction & Evaluation (CE) ARE 5.0 Mock Exam (Architect Registration Examination): ARE 5.0 Overview, Exam Prep Tips, Hotspots, Case Studies, Drag-and-Place, Solutions and Explanations
ISBN: 9781612650241

Mock California Supplemental Exam (CSE of Architect Registration Examination): CSE Overview, Exam Prep Tips, General Section and Project Scenario Section, Questions, Solutions and Explanations. **ISBN**: 9781612650159

ARE 5.0 Exam Guide Series

Practice Management (PcM) ARE 5.0 Exam Guide (Architect Registration Examination): ARE 5.0 Overview, Exam Prep Tips, Guide, and Critical Content. **ISBN**: 9781612650333

Project Management (PjM) ARE 5.0 Exam Guide (Architect Registration Examination): ARE 5.0 Overview, Exam Prep Tips, Guide, and Critical Content. **ISBN**: 9781612650418

Programming & Analysis (PA) ARE 5.0 Exam Guide (Architect Registration Examination): ARE 5.0 Overview, Exam Prep Tips, Guide, and Critical Content. **ISBN**: 9781612650487

Construction and Evaluation (CE) ARE 5 Exam Guide (Architect Registration Exam):
ARE 5.0 Overview, Exam Prep Tips, Guide, and Critical Content
ISBN: 9781612650432

Other books in the ARE 5.0 Exam Guide Series are being produced. Our goal is to produce one mock exam book *plus* one guidebook for each of the ARE 5.0 exam divisions. See the following link for the latest information:
http://www.GreenExamEducation.com

LEED Exam Guides series: Comprehensive Study Materials, Sample Questions, Mock Exam, Building LEED Certification and Going Green

LEED (Leadership in Energy and Environmental Design) is the most important trend of development, and it is revolutionizing the construction industry. It has gained tremendous momentum and has a profound impact on our environment.

From LEED Exam Guides series, you will learn how to

1. Pass the LEED Green Associate Exam and various LEED AP + exams (each book will help you with a specific LEED exam).

2. Register and certify a building for LEED certification.

3. Understand the intent for each LEED prerequisite and credit.

4. Calculate points for a LEED credit.

5. Identify the responsible party for each prerequisite and credit.

6. Earn extra credit (exemplary performance) for LEED.

7. Implement the local codes and building standards for prerequisites and credit.

8. Receive points for categories not yet clearly defined by USGBC.

There is currently NO official book on the LEED Green Associate Exam, and most of the existing books on LEED and LEED AP are too expensive and too complicated to be practical and helpful. The pocket guides in LEED Exam Guides series fill in the blanks, demystify LEED, and uncover the tips, codes, and jargon for LEED as well as the true meaning of "going green." They will set up a solid foundation and fundamental framework of LEED for you. Each book in the LEED Exam Guides series covers every aspect of one or more specific LEED rating system(s) in plain and concise language and makes this information understandable to all people.

These pocket guides are small and easy to carry around. You can read them whenever you have a few extra minutes. They are indispensable books for all people—administrators; developers; contractors; architects; landscape architects; civil, mechanical, electrical, and plumbing engineers; interns; drafters; designers; and other design professionals.

Why is the LEED Exam Guides series needed?

A number of books are available that you can use to prepare for the LEED exams:

1. *USGBC Reference Guides.* You need to select the correct version of the *Reference Guide* for your exam.

   The *USGBC Reference Guides* are comprehensive, but they give too much information. For example, *The LEED 2009 Reference Guide for Green Building Design and Construction (BD&C)* has about 700 oversized pages. Many of the calculations in the books are too detailed for the exam. They are also expensive (approximately $200 each, so most people may not buy them for their personal use, but instead, will seek to share an office copy).

   It is good to read a reference guide from cover to cover if you have the time. The problem is not too many people have time to read the whole reference guide. Even if you do read the whole guide, you may not remember the important issues to pass the LEED exam. You need to reread the material several times before you can remember much of it.

   Reading the reference guide from cover to cover without a guidebook is a difficult and inefficient way of preparing for the LEED AP Exam, because you do NOT know what USGBC and GBCI are looking for in the exam.

2. The USGBC workshops and related handouts are concise, but they do not cover extra credits (exemplary performance). The workshops are expensive, costing approximately $450 each.

3. Various books published by a third party are available on Amazon, bn.com and books.google.com. However, most of them are not very helpful.

   There are many books on LEED, but not all are useful.

   LEED Exam Guides series will fill in the blanks and become a valuable, reliable source:

   a. They will give you more information for your money. Each of the books in the LEED Exam Guides series has more information than the related USGBC workshops.

   b. They are exam-oriented and more effective than the USGBC reference guides.

   c. They are better than most, if not all, of the other third-party books. They give you comprehensive study materials, sample questions and answers, mock exams and answers, and critical information on building LEED certification and going green. Other third-party books only give you a fraction of the information.

   d. They are comprehensive yet concise. They are small and easy to carry around. You can read them whenever you have a few extra minutes.

   e. They are great timesavers. I have highlighted the important information that you need to understand and MEMORIZE. I also make some acronyms and short sentences to help you easily remember the credit names.

It should take you about 1 or 2 weeks of full-time study to pass each of the LEED exams. I have met people who have spent 40 hours to study and passed the exams.

You can find sample texts and other information on the LEED Exam Guides series in customer discussion sections under each of my book's listing on Amazon, bn.com and books.google.com.

What others are saying about *LEED GA Exam Guide* (Book 2, LEED Exam Guide series):

"Finally! A comprehensive study tool for LEED GA Prep!

"I took the 1-day Green LEED GA course and walked away with a power point binder printed in very small print—which was missing MUCH of the required information (although I didn't know it at the time). I studied my little heart out and took the test, only to fail it by 1 point. Turns out I did NOT study all the material I needed to in order to pass the test. I found this book, read it, marked it up, retook the test, and passed it with a 95%. Look, we all know the LEED GA exam is new and the resources for study are VERY limited. This one is the VERY best out there right now. I highly recommend it."
—ConsultantVA

"Complete overview for the LEED GA exam

"I studied this book for about 3 days and passed the exam … if you are truly interested in learning about the LEED system and green building design, this is a great place to start."
—K.A. Evans

"A Wonderful Guide for the LEED GA Exam

"After deciding to take the LEED Green Associate exam, I started to look for the best possible study materials and resources. From what I thought would be a relatively easy task, it turned into a tedious endeavor. I realized that there are vast amounts of third-party guides and handbooks. Since the official sites offer little to no help, it became clear to me that my best chance to succeed and pass this exam would be to find the most comprehensive study guide that would not only teach me the topics, but would also give me a great background and understanding of what LEED actually is. Once I stumbled upon Mr. Chen's book, all my needs were answered. This is a great study guide that will give the reader the most complete view of the LEED exam and all that it entails.

"The book is written in an easy-to-understand language and brings up great examples, tying the material to the real world. The information is presented in a coherent and logical way, which optimizes the learning process and does not go into details that will not be needed for the LEED Green Associate Exam, as many other guides do. This book stays dead on topic and keeps the reader interested in the material.

"I highly recommend this book to anyone that is considering the LEED Green Associate Exam. I learned a great deal from this guide, and I am feeling very confident about my chances for passing my upcoming exam."
—Pavel Geystrin

"Easy to read, easy to understand

"I have read through the book once and found it to be the perfect study guide for me. The author does a great job of helping you get into the right frame of mind for the content of the exam. I had started by studying the Green Building Design and Construction reference guide for LEED projects produced by the USGBC. That was the wrong approach, simply too much information with very little retention. At 636 pages in textbook format, it would have been a daunting task to get through it. Gang Chen breaks down the points, helping to minimize the amount of information but maximizing the content I was able to absorb. I plan on going through the book a few more times, and I now believe I have the right information to pass the LEED Green Associate Exam."
—**Brian Hochstein**

"All in one—LEED GA prep material

"Since the LEED Green Associate exam is a newer addition by USGBC, there is not much information regarding study material for this exam. When I started looking around for material, I got really confused about what material I should buy. This LEED GA guide by Gang Chen is an answer to all my worries! It is a very precise book with lots of information, like how to approach the exam, what to study and what to skip, links to online material, and tips and tricks for passing the exam. It is like the 'one stop shop' for the LEED Green Associate Exam. I think this book can also be a good reference guide for green building professionals. A must-have!"
—**SwatiD**

"An ESSENTIAL LEED GA Exam Reference Guide

"This book is an invaluable tool in preparation for the LEED Green Associate (GA) Exam. As a practicing professional in the consulting realm, I found this book to be all-inclusive of the preparatory material needed for sitting the exam. The information provides clarity to the fundamental and advanced concepts of what LEED aims to achieve. A tremendous benefit is the connectivity of the concepts with real-world applications.

"The author, Gang Chen, provides a vast amount of knowledge in a very clear, concise, and logical media. For those that have not picked up a textbook in a while, it is very manageable to extract the needed information from this book. If you are taking the exam, do yourself a favor and purchase a copy of this great guide. Applicable fields: Civil Engineering, Architectural Design, MEP, and General Land Development."
—**Edwin L. Tamang**

Note:
*Other books in the **LEED Exam Guides series** are published or in the process of being produced. At least **one book will eventually be produced for each of the LEED exams.** The series include:*

***LEED v4 Green Associate Exam Guide (LEED GA):** Comprehensive Study Materials, Sample Questions, Mock Exam, Green Building LEED Certification, and Sustainability*, LEED Exam Guide series, ArchiteG.com. Latest Edition.

LEED GA MOCK EXAMS (LEED v4): Questions, Answers, and Explanations: A Must-Have for the LEED Green Associate Exam, Green Building LEED Certification, and Sustainability, LEED Exam Guide series, ArchiteG.com. Latest Edition

LEED v4 BD&C EXAM GUIDE: A Must-Have for the LEED AP BD+C Exam: Comprehensive Study Materials, Sample Questions, Mock Exam, Green Building Design and Construction, LEED Certification, and Sustainability, LEED Exam Guide series, ArchiteG.com. Latest Edition.

LEED v4 BD&C MOCK EXAMS: Questions, Answers, and Explanations: A Must-Have for the LEED AP BD+C Exam, Green Building LEED Certification, and Sustainability, LEED Exam Guide series, ArchiteG.com. Latest Edition.

LEED v4 ID&C Exam Guide: A Must-Have for the LEED AP ID+C Exam: Study Materials, Sample Questions, Green Interior Design and Construction, Green Building LEED Certification, and Sustainability, LEED Exam Guide series, ArchiteG.com. Latest Edition.

LEED v4 AP ID+C MOCK EXAM: Questions, Answers, and Explanations: A Must-Have for the LEED AP ID+C Exam, Green Building LEED Certification, and Sustainability. LEED Exam Guide series, ArchiteG.com. Latest Edition.

LEED v4 AP O+M MOCK EXAM: Questions, Answers, and Explanations: A Must-Have for the LEED AP O+M Exam, Green Building LEED Certification, and Sustainability. LEED Exam Guide series, ArchiteG.com. Latest Edition.

LEED v4 O&M EXAM GUIDE: A Must-Have for the LEED AP O+M Exam: Comprehensive Study Materials, Sample Questions, Mock Exam, Green Building Operations and Maintenance, LEED Certification, and Sustainability, LEED Exam Guide series, ArchiteG.com. Latest Edition.

LEED v4 HOMES EXAM GUIDE: A Must-Have for the LEED AP Homes Exam: Comprehensive Study Materials, Sample Questions, Mock Exam, Green Building LEED Certification, and Sustainability, LEED Exam Guide series, ArchiteG.com. Latest Edition.

LEED v4 ND EXAM GUIDE: A Must-Have for the LEED AP Neighborhood Development Exam: Comprehensive Study Materials, Sample Questions, Mock Exam, Green Building LEED Certification, and Sustainability, LEED Exam Guide series, ArchiteG.com. Latest Edition.

How to order these books:
You can order the books listed above at:
http://www.GreenExamEducation.com

OR
http://www.ArchiteG.com

Building Construction

Project Management, Construction Administration, Drawings, Specs, Detailing Tips, Schedules, Checklists, and Secrets Others Don't Tell You (Architectural Practice Simplified, 2nd edition)

Learn the Tips, Become One of Those Who Know Building Construction and Architectural Practice, and Thrive!

For architectural practice and building design and construction industry, there are two kinds of people: those who know, and those who don't. The tips of building design and construction and project management have been undercover—until now.

Most of the existing books on building construction and architectural practice are too expensive, too complicated, and too long to be practical and helpful. This book simplifies the process to make it easier to understand and uncovers the tips of building design and construction and project management. It sets up a solid foundation and fundamental framework for this field. It covers every aspect of building construction and architectural practice in plain and concise language and introduces it to all people. Through practical case studies, it demonstrates the efficient and proper ways to handle various issues and problems in architectural practice and building design and construction industry.

It is for ordinary people and aspiring young architects as well as seasoned professionals in the construction industry. For ordinary people, it uncovers the tips of building construction; for aspiring architects, it works as a construction industry survival guide and a guidebook to shorten the process in mastering architectural practice and climbing up the professional ladder; for seasoned architects, it has many checklists to refresh their memory. It is an indispensable reference book for ordinary people, architectural students, interns, drafters, designers, seasoned architects, engineers, construction administrators, superintendents, construction managers, contractors, and developers.

You will learn:
1. How to develop your business and work with your client.
2. The entire process of building design and construction, including programming, entitlement, schematic design, design development, construction documents, bidding, and construction administration.
3. How to coordinate with governing agencies, including a county's health department and a city's planning, building, fire, public works departments, etc.
4. How to coordinate with your consultants, including soils, civil, structural, electrical, mechanical, plumbing engineers, landscape architects, etc.
5. How to create and use your own checklists to do quality control of your construction documents.
6. How to use various logs (i.e., RFI log, submittal log, field visit log, etc.) and lists (contact list, document control list, distribution list, etc.) to organize and simplify your work.
7. How to respond to RFI, issue CCDs, review change orders, submittals, etc.
8. How to make your architectural practice a profitable and successful business.

Planting Design Illustrated
A Must-Have for Landscape Architecture: A Holistic Garden Design Guide with Architectural and Horticultural Insight, and Ideas from Famous Gardens in Major Civilizations

One of the most significant books on landscaping!

This is one of the most comprehensive books on planting design. It fills in the blanks of the field and introduces poetry, painting, and symbolism into planting design. It covers in detail the two major systems of planting design: formal planting design and naturalistic planting design. It has numerous line drawings and photos to illustrate the planting design concepts and principles. Through in-depth discussions of historical precedents and practical case studies, it uncovers the fundamental design principles and concepts, as well as the underpinning philosophy for planting design. It is an indispensable reference book for landscape architecture students, designers, architects, urban planners, and ordinary garden lovers.

What Others Are Saying about _Planting Design Illustrated_ ...

"I found this book to be absolutely fascinating. You will need to concentrate while reading it, but the effort will be well worth your time."
—Bobbie Schwartz, former president of APLD (Association of Professional Landscape Designers) and author of _The Design Puzzle: Putting the Pieces Together_.

"This is a book that you have to read, and it is more than well worth your time. Gang Chen takes you well beyond what you will learn in other books about basic principles like color, texture, and mass."
—Jane Berger, editor & publisher of gardendesignonline

"As a longtime consumer of gardening books, I am impressed with Gang Chen's inclusion of new information on planting design theory for Chinese and Japanese gardens. Many gardening books discuss the beauty of Japanese gardens, and a few discuss the unique charms of Chinese gardens, but this one explains how Japanese and Chinese history, as well as geography and artistic traditions, bear on the development of each country's style. The material on traditional Western garden planting is thorough and inspiring, too. _Planting Design Illustrated_ definitely rewards repeated reading and study. Any garden designer will read it with profit."
—Jan Whitner, editor of the _Washington Park Arboretum Bulletin_

"Enhanced with an annotated bibliography and informative appendices, _Planting Design Illustrated_ offers an especially "reader friendly" and practical guide that makes it a very strongly recommended addition to personal, professional, academic, and community library gardening & landscaping reference collection and supplemental reading list."
—Midwest Book Review

"Where to start? *Planting Design Illustrated* is, above all, fascinating and refreshing! Not something the lay reader encounters every day, the book presents an unlikely topic in an easily digestible, easy-to-follow way. It is superbly organized with a comprehensive table of contents, bibliography, and appendices. The writing, though expertly informative, maintains its accessibility throughout and is a joy to read. The detailed and beautiful illustrations expanding on the concepts presented were my favorite portion. One of the finest books I've encountered in this contest in the past 5 years."
—**Writer's Digest 16th Annual International Self-Published Book Awards Judge's Commentary**

"The work in my view has incredible application to planting design generally and a system approach to what is a very difficult subject to teach, at least in my experience. Also featured is a very beautiful philosophy of garden design principles bordering poetry. It's my strong conviction that this work needs to see the light of day by being published for the use of professionals, students & garden enthusiasts."
—**Donald C. Brinkerhoff, FASLA, chairman and CEO of Lifescapes International, Inc.**

Index

Notes

Notes